Intended For Oneness

*The Meaning, Fulfillment, and
Administration of Marriage*

by

ReVoe S. Hill III

(Bud)

Richard - We have
been blessed to Know
you and your family

Blessings
— ReVoe Hill III

Edited by Randall S. Newton and ReVoe S. Hill III

Special thanks to Pastor Rennie McCormick and River of Grace Church, Tonasket, WA; and Pastor Tilford Hansen and New Life Centre, Okanogan, WA.

Cover photo courtesy of Tim Davis, thank you for your generosity. www.nwphototrail.com

Endorsement:

This is not a run of the mill book on Christian marriage. If you are looking for practical keys on how not to annoy your spouse or how to improve your emotional IQ, your choices of books are numerous. If you want a book on Biblical Marriage which presents the complete story, the mystery, then you have the right book; *Intended For Oneness* by ReVoe S. Hill III.

This comprehensive study on marriage is beyond anything I've read on the subject. Hill has established a foundation in biblical studies for marriage which future works can build upon. Hill writes, "The Mosaic Law forbids a husband to remarry his former wife yet God promises to do it." If you understand this statement, this book provides the needed background so you can teach it. If you are perplexed about this statement, then, you need the book. This book takes us beyond fixing troublesome marriages. It takes us to the heart of God behind the institution. We learn why marriage exists and why it is imperative we get it right.

Every Pastor and church leader must read this book. Why?, because the church needs this teaching. Why?, because the church is to model marriage to the world. Buy this book! Read this book! Study this book! Give copies to your friends and your pastor. This is a one of a kind book and I highly endorse it. This is a classic for the generations.

Dr. Stan Newton,

Missionary and Bible Teacher

TABLE OF CONTENTS

PART 1: THE MEANING OF MARRIAGE

Introduction

You know the line. You can probably recite it perfectly. To those who profess Christ, to those meeting in the auditoriums of every Christian church, and probably in every Christian wedding believers are bound to hear these words:

> *Genesis 2:24: Therefore a man shall leave his father and mother and be joined to his wife, and they shall become one flesh. (New King James Version)*

This scripture truly remains foundational to Christian heritage in both the spiritual/ figurative understanding and the physical/literal application; yet, to say that Christianity holds the exclusive rights to marriage reflects a great ignorance. We know that throughout history and in all cultures to varying degrees marriage is accepted if not defined as being between a man and a woman. I accept this assumption in order to abstain from sociological application and focus solely on the truth and revelation of the scriptures. I write this book to the Christian church, the Body of Christ.

In the growing hostility of today's culture toward Godly living, efforts to dismantle and redefine marriage successfully influences the farthest points of our society. State and local governments, corporations, celebrities, lobbyists, et. al., see the marriage debate as a profitable opportunity to throw off the bonds of righteousness and embrace the enlightened faith of this New Age. Grievously, some church leaders with their congregations and even whole denominations deny Christ to embrace and promote the marriage covenant to include homosexuality. However, I find it unfortunate that even among proponents standing to uphold the truth about marriage, the richness and fullness of scripture yields to history, tradition and statistics. My intention in this book is to provide a fundamental scriptural teaching regarding the following questions:

- What is marriage?
- Why was marriage given?
- What connects marriage to our salvation?
- How does the Christian church serve the Kingdom of God in marriage?

Before I move on you need to understand that this book is not directed to those that reject Christ and His gospel. This message is directed to Christ's church, so the statements that I make are going to be in reference to Christ's church. In 1 Corinthians 5 Paul addresses an issue of sexual immorality in the Corinthian church so offensive even the pagans avoid it. The Corinthians not only permitted this incestuous relationship, but they took pride in their open mindedness, their freedom and graciousness. Addressing this perversion in the church, Paul says in verses 9-13:

> *1 Corinthians 5:9-13: (emphasis added) [9]I wrote to you in my epistle not to keep company with sexually immoral people. [10]Yet I certainly did not mean with the sexually immoral people of this world, or with the covetous, or extortioners, or idolaters, since then you would need to go out of the world. [And which would be a direct contradiction to the command of Christ to "go into the world."] [11]But now I have written to you **not to keep company with anyone named a brother**, who is sexually immoral, or covetous, or an idolater, or a reviler, or a drunkard, or an extortioner—not even to eat with such a person. [12]For what have I to do with judging those who are outside? Do you not judge those who are inside?*

13But those who are outside God judges. Therefore 'put away from yourselves, the evil person.' (NKJV)

This scripture reminds us that Christ obligates His church to judge the actions of those in it, marked both by identifying ungodly activity and cutting off those that engage in such activity. The result of such judgment is to strengthen the body and therefore glorify Christ. If the one judged repents, after the protection of the church lifts, then restoration between the body and its member takes place. Christ receives glory. If the "evil person" does not repent then the church remains undefiled before God for putting away evil from among its members. Christ receives glory.

God judges those outside the church. Christians must understand the sins and the perversions of the ungodly are just a reflection of the fallen nature. In this way God covers us and frees us to be among the ungodly in love, mercy and grace; to be in the world not of the world. This freedom allows us to perform the ministry of reconciliation. In 2 Corinthians 5:14, Paul writes this:

*2 Corinthians 5:14-21: (emphasis added) 14**For the love of Christ compels us**, because we judge thus: that if One died for all then all died; 15and He died for all, that those who live should live no longer for themselves, but for Him who died for them and rose again. 16Therefore, from now on, we regard no one according to the flesh. Even though we have known Christ according to the flesh, yet now we know Him thus no longer. 17Therefore, if anyone is in Christ, he is a new creation; old things have passed away; behold all things have become new. 18Now all things are of God, who has **reconciled** us to Himself through Jesus Christ, and has given us the **ministry of reconciliation**, 19that is, that God was in Christ reconciling the world to Himself, not imputing their trespasses to them, and has committed to us the **word of reconciliation**. 20Now* *then, we are ambassadors for Christ, as though God were pleading through us: **we implore you on Christ's behalf, be reconciled to God.** [21]For He made Him who knew no sin to be sin for us, that we might become the righteousness of God in Him. (NKJV)*

God authorizes His church to bring the hope and life of the gospel to mankind in order to reconcile mankind to God. God, through Christ, performed His part of reconciliation by removing the object of our offense toward Him. He forgave our offense by bearing it Himself through the Body of Christ as Paul says, "*[21]For He made Him who knew no sin to be sin for us, that we might become the righteousness of God in Him.*" Yet forgiveness of offense only covers part, though it is the largest part, of reconciliation. We must still respond to God by embracing the New Covenant established by the death, burial, and resurrection of the Lord Jesus Christ. Only then can one say "I am reconciled to God and have become the righteousness of God through Christ." To this point of becoming the righteousness of God I write this book. Once reconciled to God, He then liberates us from the Law of Death and binds us to the Law of the New Covenant, the Law of the Spirit. The Law of the Spirit convicts of sin and completes the perfect work by teaching us how to put to death the sinful, perverted nature and increase in God's nature. Where the Law of Death is contained within the whole of the Old Testament, The Law of the Spirit is found in three simple commandments and three simple ordinances:

The three Laws of the New Covenant, the Law of the Spirit:

1. Love the Lord with all your heart, soul, mind and strength. (Mat. 22:37)
2. Love your neighbor as yourself. (Mat. 22:39, Mat. 7:12, Rom. 13:8-10)
3. Love the brethren as Christ loved you. (John 13:34, 1Tim. 1:5-8)

The three ordinances of abstinence or commands given by the Apostles: (Acts 15:28-29, Acts 21:25, Rev. 2:18-20)

1. Abstain from food offered to idols.
2. Abstain from strangled meats.
3. Abstain from sexual immorality.

The substance of the Law is love; love for God and love for one another.

Now when those who have the knowledge of Christ choose to fully embrace and support those things that are openly offensive to their Lord and Savior, the rest of the body has an obligation to judge them. Even to the point of putting them out of the fellowship. In this book I intend to give a clear understanding of marriage so that we can rightly discern and reject the perversions against it. The marriage covenant is so basic and foundational to the plans and purposes of God that without it, salvation and reconciliation do not exist. Without marriage redemption fails. Without marriage healing descends into illusion. Without marriage the gifts remain withheld. Without marriage eternal life gives place to myth, and hope fades. Marriage must always stand as a cornerstone of our faith.

CHAPTER 1   The Man Alone

We often think of marriage as starting in the garden. But in truth it started long before the Garden of Eden. Let's go to Genesis 2:18 in the creation story:

> *Genesis 2:18-24: ¹⁸And the Lord God said, "It is not good that man should be alone; I will make him a helper comparable to him." ¹⁹Out of the ground the Lord God formed every beast of the field and every bird of the air, and brought them to Adam to see what he would call them. And whatever Adam called each living creature, that was its name. ²⁰So Adam gave names to all cattle, to the birds of the air, and to every beast of the field. But for Adam there was not found a helper comparable to him.²¹ And the Lord God caused a deep sleep to fall on Adam, and he slept; and He took one of his ribs, and closed up the flesh in its place. ²²Then the rib which the Lord God had taken from man He made into a woman, and He brought her to the man. ²³And Adam said: "This is now bone of my bones and flesh of my flesh; She shall be called Woman, Because she was taken out of Man." ²⁴Therefore a man shall leave his father and mother and be joined to his wife, and they shall become one flesh. (NKJV)*

We recognize this passage as cited in most wedding ceremonies performed in churches today. At some point, in many weddings, the Officiant comes to this scripture. And so many times the reading stops right there and the listener is left with a statement requiring an assumption: "This is the way that God ordained it, and that's just the way it is." Unfortunately, this statement requires us as believers to accept the truth of marriage as beyond our understanding, so don't try, just accept and obey. I do accept and obey, but I also hunger to know and understand. Paul said in Romans 10:17,

"So then faith comes by hearing and hearing by the word of God."
(NKJV) Peter expounds further in 2 Peter 1:

> *2 Peter 1:2-8: (emphasis added) ²Grace and peace be*
> *multiplied to you through **the knowledge of God** and of Jesus*
> *our Lord, ³according as His divine power has given to us all*
> *things that pertain to life and godliness, through the*
> ***knowledge of Him** who has called us to glory and virtue,*
> *⁴through which He has given to us exceedingly great and*
> *precious promises, so that by these you might be **partakers***
> ***of the divine nature**, having escaped the corruption that is*
> *in the world through lust. ⁵But also in this very thing,*
> *bringing in all diligence, filling out your faith with virtue, and*
> *with virtue, **knowledge**; ⁶and with **knowledge** self-control,*
> *and with self-control, patience, and with patience, godliness,*
> *⁷and with godliness, brotherly kindness, and with brotherly*
> *kindness, love. ⁸For if these things are in you and abound, they*
> *make you to be neither idle nor unfruitful in the **knowledge***
> ***of our Lord Jesus Christ**." (Modern King James Version)*

Peter teaches that faith, not knowledge, must be the first step
in partaking of the divine nature. Then adding virtue or upright
conduct to what you believe, which is praiseworthy. From
there we add knowledge and so forth. The point I believe Peter
makes centers around God's intent to teach us who He is.
However, only by believing the word of God and conducting
yourself in a manner comparable to your faith does God impart
knowledge of Himself. So to partake of the divine nature
requires me to increase in my knowledge of God. The increase
of knowledge depends on faith in what the Word says and in
my conduct. God is under no obligation to reveal Himself to
man. However, when we believe what He says and add virtue
to faith He brings understanding to what we believe. By faith
we accept that marriage is from the beginning, by faith we also
believe that marriage has purpose.

At this point proponents of traditional marriage may fall back on tradition and statistics. Someone may ask, "Why would God create marriage? What makes marriage important to God?" The proponent may answer, "Well, for the purpose of reproduction." However, nature proves that you can reproduce without being married. Society demonstrates that you can reproduce without marriage. So that's not the answer. Or the proponent may say, "Because marriage is the foundation of the family unit." Well, nature proves that you can have a family unit without being married. From a forest of trees, to a pack of wolves, to a pod of whales, to a flock of birds, the family unit of parents and offspring exists without marriage. After all, the command to be fruitful and multiply applied to all creation not just to mankind. Maybe the proponent says, "Marriage is the cornerstone of civilization; the corruption of marriage is the breakdown of civilization." Although I accept this, why I agree may be for different reasons than many traditional marriage proponents.

The introduction of man into creation was a unique and singular event. In the creation story God made multiples. Yet when He created man He said, "Let Us make man in Our image." and He made one human, unique and singular. Though all creation came into existence by the power of God's spoken word, God formed man by His own hand and gave man His own breath. Eve did not come from the earth but from man; unique and singular.

After placing man in the garden God said, "It's not good that man is alone." That statement should raise all kinds of red flags, or it does for the enemies of the gospel. They may ask, "How could God, who knows all things and always does good admit from the very beginning of creation that He did something not good. Why would God do that? Did He screw up? Was he just making things up as He went along?" Did God make a mistake? No. Surely He knew what He was doing, right?

Yes. To the corrupt and foolish heart, God hides His plans but to those that believe He opens the heart and mind to understand.

Returning to the creation story, God said, "Let Us make man in Our image" and He made one. God is one, one God and one man. In Genesis 1 God gives the command for man to reproduce:

> Genesis 1:27-28: 27So God created man in His own image; in the image of God He created him; male and female He created them. 28Then God blessed them, and God said to them, "Be fruitful and multiply; fill the earth and subdue it; have dominion over the fish of the sea, over the birds of the air, and over every living thing that moves on the earth." (NKJV)

Though God intended for man to be male and female only the male existed in the beginning. God intended for man to reproduce yet in the beginning only the male existed. In the beginning only God existed and God is one; in the beginning God created man in His image and man was one.

> Genesis 2:18: And the Lord God said, "It is not good that man should be alone; I will make a helper comparable to him." (NKJV)

God said, "It is not good that man be alone..." Why does God show such concern for the loneliness of man, when God made only one? Through all creation, God made big families. He made them male and female, and told them to reproduce. Then God made man and told him to reproduce, yet He only made one. It was God that noticed Adam was alone. It was God that said, "It is not good that you are alone..." Adam didn't come to God and say, "I'm alone, I need somebody." God said, "You're alone, and that's not good." God wants to tell us why He does what He does. When Jesus spoke to His disciples about His parables He said this in Matthew 13:

Matthew 13:13-16: (emphasis added) [13]*Therefore I speak to them in parables, because seeing they see not, and hearing they hear not; nor do they understand.* [14]*And in them is fulfilled the prophecy of Isaiah which said, "By hearing you shall hear and shall not understand; and seeing you shall see and shall not perceive;* [15]***for this people's heart has become gross, and their ears are dull of hearing, and they have closed their eyes***, *lest at any time they should see with their eyes and hear with their ears and should understand with their heart, and should be converted, and I should heal them."* [16]***But blessed are your eyes, for they see; and your ears, for they hear.*** *(MKJV)*

Jesus spoke in parables to hide His meaning from those that rejected Him; but to those that loved Him, He revealed the meaning of the parables. God wants us to know and He takes great pleasure in revealing the mysteries of His kingdom to all that love Him. In understanding God's kingdom, we find out more about who He is, but we also find out more about who we are. So seek and you will find. Knock and the door will be opened. Ask and He will answer. Okay, here's the question. Why would God create a single man and later condemn the man's solitude as not good?

CHAPTER 2   Alone Among Creation

Paul answers the question asked in the previous chapter: "Why did God create a single man and later condemn the man's solitude as not good?" In Ephesians 5 starting in verse 22, Paul says this:

> *Ephesians 5:22-31:* [22]*Wives, submit to your own husbands, as to the Lord.* [23]*For the husband is head of the wife, as also Christ is head of the church; and He is the Savior of the body.* [24]*Therefore, just as the church is subject to Christ, so let the wives be to their own husbands in everything.* [25]*Husbands, love your wives, just as Christ also loved the church and gave Himself for her,* [26]*that He might sanctify and cleanse her with the washing of water by the word,* [27]*that He might present her to Himself a glorious church, not having spot or wrinkle or any such thing, but that she should be holy and without blemish.* [28]*So husbands ought to love their own wives as their own bodies; he who loves his wife loves himself.* [29]*For no one ever hated his own flesh, but nourishes and cherishes it, just as the Lord does the church.* [30]*For we are members of His body, of His flesh and of His bones.* [31]*"For this reason a man shall leave his father and mother and be joined to his wife, and the two shall become one flesh."* (NKJV)

How often does this text get used to accuse Christian wives of not submitting to their husbands? How often does this text get used to accuse Christian husbands of not loving their wives? How often have we Christians viewed this text as being about us. We assume it addresses our relationships toward one another. So wives, you need to submit to your husbands, and husbands you need to be more loving toward your wives. Paul gives the true meaning of this text in verse 31-32:

Ephesians 5:31-32: "*³¹For this reason a man shall leave his father and mother and be joined to his wife, and the two shall become one flesh." This is a great mystery, but I speak concerning Christ and His church.* (NKJV)

Paul quotes directly out of Genesis 2:31, *For this reason a man shall leave his father and mother and be joined to his wife, and the two shall become one flesh.* At this point it may be beneficial to just step back and look at this text again from the perspective of God's great genius and love. As flesh we often struggle against our limitations as defined by time. Add to that the temptation to see the scriptures as a manual to Godly living and we can so easily miss the beauty of God's genius.

Our fleshly limitations cause us to think literally, lineally, chronologically. Yet no such limitations impact God. We perceive the Scriptures as occurring at the beginning of time and moving chronologically. However, the creation account claims God created time (evening and morning were the first day), so God exists outside of time. When we perceive the Scriptures as a manual, then we miss the greatest foundational truth of all the Scriptures: the Scriptures testify of Christ. The Scriptures were not given to man as a manual teaching him how not to offend God. The Scriptures remain a testament to God's great brilliance, His deep love, and His intentionality.

The teaching of Paul in Ephesians 5 gives deeper revelation into God's genius. The church may teach Ephesians 5 as a parallel to what happened in the Garden, an example to follow in understanding the meaning of marriage. However, the church would be wrong. Ephesians 5 does not teach us about the relationship between husbands and wives. Ephesians 5 teaches us about the plan of God concealed from the very beginning. The concealed plan, or mystery according to Paul, revealed in Ephesians, is God wanted a helpmate for Himself and purposed through time to get her. Christ and His church is the revealing of that mystery. The reality, substance, and revelation of the Scriptures center on God and His intent to create a wife through the work of Christ. Therefore, the events beginning in the garden and moving through all the Scriptures, including the teaching on marriage, only shadow the reality. When Paul teaches about husbands loving your wives because it is a reflection of the mystery revealed, he means Christ and His church. So what is the definition of marriage? Marriage is nothing more than the reflection of God's intent towards mankind.

Paul, referring back to creation in verse 31 tells us that the introduction of Eve to Adam is about the joining of Christ to His church. So if Christ represents Adam, of whom God said, "*It is not good that the man is alone*," then the church represents Eve of whom God said, "*I will make a helper comparable to him.*" Marriage unites a unique creation, compatible and complimentary to the creator, God, who stands great and awesome, yet alone among His creation. How strange to think of God as alone among His creation. We hear of projections in the media of immense numbers of stars in our galaxy with even greater numbers of planets. Yet these numbers are miniscule compared to the numbers of galaxies, stars, planets, and great wonders in the unknown universe. God creates all of it by the word of His mouth, and sustains it all by His power. He comes to this planet and brings life. He speaks, "*Let there be birds, fouls of the air.*" That's all He says, and yet we have such variety of species of birds. He says, "*Let there be beast on the earth.*" And we have this variety of land animals. Just by a word and a thought. He creates this incredible wonder, surrounded by all of His creation, yet God remains alone. God said, "*It's not good that I am alone. I will create for me, a helpmate. I will make a wife comparable to me.*" God found nothing, in all of creation that could fill the role of helpmate.

The Apostle Paul calls this a "great mystery." It was the role of the apostles to reveal the mysteries of God. And Paul acting as an apostle says, "*This is a great mystery but*" he says "*I speak of Christ and His church.*" When the word "mystery" is used in the New Testament, it refers to the revealing of hidden things from the Old Testament. If Paul refers to the marriage of Christ and His church as a "great mystery," then the true meaning of marriage remained hidden in the Old Testament. The "great mystery" could be defined as this: all of heaven knew that God was alone. All of heaven knew that God wanted a helpmate. God stood alone, yet wanting a wife. How do you bridge that gap? How can the Creator immortal, immeasurable, and supreme bridge the gap between Himself and His creation to make a helper comparable to Him? How can He do that? How can God create something from His creation that compares to Himself? How can God take something physical and natural, change it into a helpmate that is spiritual, sharing in the same attributes as God Himself. Still struggling with the question? Maybe to ask it in terms of unity would be helpful. How does God become one with His creation; not just in thought but also in body and purpose? The Gospel of John communicates this clearly:

> *John 14:10-17:* *¹⁰Do you not believe that I am in the Father and the Father in Me? The Words that I speak to you I do not speak of Myself, but the Father who dwells in Me, He does the works.¹¹Believe Me that I am in the Father and the Father in Me, or else believe Me for the very works themselves. ¹²Truly, truly, I say to you, He who believes on Me, the works that I do he shall do also, and greater works than these he shall do, because I go to My Father. ¹³And whatever you may ask in My name, that I will do, so that the Father may be glorified in the Son. ¹⁴If you ask anything in My name, I will do it. ¹⁵If you love Me, keep My commandments. ¹⁶And I will pray the Father, and He shall give you another Comforter, so that He may be*

with you forever, [17]the Spirit of Truth, whom the world cannot receive because it does not see Him nor know Him. But you know Him, for He dwells with you and shall be in you. (MKJV)

God no longer wanted to be alone, so he purposed to create a wife for Himself. God established the marriage covenant between man and woman to show His intentions to marry. Marriage can only occur between a man and woman because it reflects God's intentions to marry. God determined, established, and purposed it before he formed the world. Therefore, since marriage comes from God and not nature, it stands as supernatural in concept and practice. Man and woman coming together to form a covenant, a pact, a life choice, for the purpose of joining as equals. Two become one. *"For this reason a man shall leave his father and mother and be joined to his wife, and they shall be one flesh."* That does not happen in nature. Marriage is supernatural, a gift passed down to all mankind.

How God, through Christ, brought salvation reveals the mystery behind Eve's creation. At the creation of Adam and Eve, where did Eve come from? Did God speak her into existence? Did God make her the way He made Adam? God created Eve differently. God's creation of all things on the earth remained consistent to the environment of the earth, including Adam. He made Adam from the earth why not make Eve from the earth? God again created a unique and solitary being. He took from the man, from his side, a part of the man, and from the man formed woman. He then presented her to the man and called them "man"—oneness. Oneness defines God, oneness defines marriage.

How does marriage in the garden reflect God's desire for oneness? God took from Adam, a part of Adam, and from that part created a woman. Man had been divided in two, and then

He brought the two together again to make one. Nothing in creation could meet the need of oneness with Adam. His helpmate could only come from his own body. In the final picture of the garden, we see the relationship between God and man. God and man had relationship but not oneness. We know God wanted oneness but creation could not stand in equality with the Creator. When man separated himself from God then the relationship failed. God showed that only by joining with creation could He create for Himself from Himself a wife compatible to Himself. Christ fulfilled and defined the mystery of Adam and Eve. Christ the Son of God and the Son of Man, through the work of redemption, made it possible for all who believed on Him to live in oneness with God.

The New Testament is full of this restoration in relationship. If we come into the New Covenant established by the body and blood of Christ then we are in Christ and therefore in God. We attain oneness with God in the marriage covenant. God made marriage precious, sacred, holy, powerful and transcendent. Not of itself, but because it reveals God's intention to be one with man. Marriage holds a place of such great significance that the Lord Jesus Christ said:

> Matthew 19:4-6: *⁴And He answered and said to them, Have you not read that He who made them at the beginning "made them male and female," ⁵and said, For this cause a man shall leave father and mother and shall cling to his wife, and the two of them shall be one flesh? ⁶Therefore they are no longer two, but one flesh. Therefore what God has joined together, let not man separate. (MKJV)*

"Therefore what God has joined together, let no man separate." Scripture does not speak this way concerning anything else. He says, "This is mine. Don't touch it." God conceived it, God defined it and God defends it.

CHAPTER 3   Marriage and Inheritance

A common thread in the creation account begins with Genesis 1 verses 11-12:

> *11 Then God said, "Let the earth bring forth grass, the herb that yields seed, and the fruit tree that yields fruit according to its kind, whose seed is in itself, on the earth"; and it was so. 12 And the earth brought forth grass, the herb that yields seed according to its kind, and the tree that yields fruit, whose seed is in itself according to its kind. And God saw that it was good." (NKJV)*

Let's go to verse 22:

> *22 And God blessed them, saying, "Be fruitful and multiply, and fill the waters in the seas, and let birds multiply on the earth." (NKJV)*

God commands creation to be fruitful and multiply and fill the earth, so nature must follow God's command to bear offspring. Now let's go to verses 27-28:

> *27 So God created man in His own image; in the image of God He created him; male and female he created them. 28 Then God blessed them, and God said to them, "Be fruitful and multiply; fill the earth and subdue it; have dominion over the fish of the sea, over the birds of the air, and over every living thing that moves on the earth." (NKJV)*

So God blesses them and says, "Be fruitful, multiply, and have dominion over my creation." This blessing contains two parts, reproduction and dominion over nature.

God commands man to reproduce like all the rest of creation. If, according to Paul, the creation of Adam and Eve

communicates the revealing of Christ and His church, then
God's command to reproduce reflects His own desire to
reproduce. Therefore, we must accept that God intended—
from before time began—to reproduce after Himself. If again,
according to Paul, the creation of Adam and Eve is meant to
communicate the revealing of Christ and His church, then God's
commands to reproduce must also reflect His desire to
reproduce after His own kind.

So God desired to have descendants? God desires to have a
family? Well yes, yes He does; hard to understand? You know,
if God made us in His image and we want to have a family, then
could such desire to reproduce just be the reflection of God's
intention for Himself? It's perfectly natural. However, we also
want to have something to pass onto our children, we want to
build something that we can give them. This desire to pass on
an inheritance is also something that is unique to mankind.
You don't see that in nature. In nature, among animals
especially, once the brood gets to a certain point, they're
kicked out of the nest. Go make your own way. Don't come
back. That's it. There's nothing to give, there's nothing to pass
on, except genetics. But among men, we have this compulsion
to reproduce and pass something on. It could be monetary,
property, or some kind of a heritage. Even those who lack
property want to leave advice from their life's experience.
Passing on an inheritance does not occur in nature, only among
mankind. And to not leave something to pass on is most
unfortunate if not tragic. So then, can we say that man's desire
to pass on an inheritance to his children reflects God's heart
toward man? Paul talks about this in Galatians chapters 3 and
4.

*Galatians 3:26-29: ²⁶For you are all sons of God through faith
in Christ Jesus. ²⁷For as many of you as were baptized into
Christ have put on Christ. ²⁸There is neither Jew nor Greek,
there is neither slave nor free, there is neither male nor*

female; for you are all one in Christ Jesus. ²⁹And if you are Christ's then you are Abraham's seed, and heirs according to the promise. (NKJV)

He continues in chapter 4:1-6:

¹Now I say that the heir, as long as he is a child, does not differ at all from a slave, though he is master of all,² but is under guardians and stewards until the time appointed by the father.³ Even so we, when we were children, were in bondage under the elements of the world.⁴ But when the fullness of the time had come, God sent forth His Son, born of a woman, born under the law,⁵ to redeem those who were under the law, that we might receive the adoption as sons. ⁶And because you are sons, God has sent forth the Spirit of His Son into your hearts, crying out, "Abba, Father!"⁷Therefore you are no longer a slave but a son, and if a son, then an heir of God through Christ. (NKJV)

Once again we see the revelation of Christ bridging the gap between God and His creation. Christ makes possible the joining of the father and His creation to create children and heirs.

God wanted children that could receive His inheritance. He creates all of this in the physical, but reveals it through Christ to be fulfilled in the spiritual. Again, that can't be hard to understand. A man can live his life complete in himself without wife or children. A woman can live a full life without husband or children. Yet, for the dominant majority of all people, we desire a mate to be joined to. From that union we produce children in the hope of leaving something of ourselves with them. So then, can it be so difficult to accept God wanting a wife and children out of desire instead of need or lack? God wants a wife and children upon which to pour out His love. Children are a lot of work. They take a lot of resources. They take a lot of patience. They take your youth. But the satisfaction of having someone to pass on something, to give of oneself, is rewarding. It's worth it. This also cannot be found in nature; it comes from God and must be seen as supernatural.

The problem with using the physical to explain the spiritual is that eventually the physical reaches a certain limit, but God's reality extends beyond physical limitations. Time, age and decay affect neither God nor his plans. He spent millennia bringing mankind from Genesis to Christ. Dealing with His people Israel, dealing with the gentiles, all for the purpose of bringing them to Christ. What amazes me about marriage is that God gave marriage to all men. Marriage not only belonged to Israel or the Jews but to all nations. Marriage became part of every culture in various forms. God from the very beginning gifted marriage to all peoples so that when the time came, it would be the mystery revealed of His intentions. God intended to have a wife, a bride that would share in His pursuits. From their unity God would reproduce children resembling Himself; heirs to pass on an inheritance.

God blessed man and commanded him to fill the earth, but He also commanded man to have dominion over the earth. In Matthew 25 Jesus talks about the coming of His kingdom:

> *Matthew 25:31-40: *[31]*When the Son of Man comes in His glory, and all the holy angels with Him, then He will sit on the throne of His glory. *[32]*All the nations will be gathered before Him, and He will separate them one from another, as a shepherd divides his sheep from the goats.*

Notice Jesus' does not refer to Jews, He refers to all nations being gathered to Him.

> [33]*And He will set the sheep on His right hand, but the goats on the left. *[34]* Then the king will say to those on His right hand, "Come, you blessed of My Father, inherit the kingdom*

prepared for you from the foundation of the world; ³⁵for I was hungry and you gave Me food; I was thirsty and you gave Me drink; I was a stranger and you took me in; ³⁶I was naked and you clothed Me; I was sick and you visited Me; I was in prison and you came to Me. ³⁷ Then the righteous will answer Him, saying, "Lord when did we see You hungry and feed You, or thirsty and give You drink? ³⁸When did we see You a stranger and take You in, or naked and clothe You? ³⁹Or when did we see You sick, or in prison, and come to You?" ⁴⁰And the King will answer and say to them, "Assuredly, I say to you, inasmuch as you did it to one of the least of these My brethren, you did it to Me." (NKJV)

Jesus identifies the righteous as the sheep on His right hand. These righteous are gathered from all the nations and given this reward, "Come, you blessed of My Father, inherit the kingdom prepared for you from the foundation of the world." Before the foundation of the world, the Father prepared an inheritance to be given with Kingdom authority. Just as He established the marriage covenant before the foundation of the world, so he provided for his righteous ones before the world's founding.

How great is God's brilliance, His wisdom and foresight. How great is His love to provide a way for all men to become His righteous ones and receive kingdom authority laid aside since before ancient days. God does not conduct Himself flippantly. He structures and implements His plans according to law. We must continue to remind ourselves that kings and despots see themselves as gods yet conduct themselves as mere men, whimsical and unaccountable. Yet God is not a man; God does everything according to law. If God established marriage before creation, then we must understand marriage as law. If God established before the foundation of the world a trust for His seed, you must understand He secures it by law. And through time, from the first evening and morning through today and on to infinity, God does everything by law. Everything must be done according to law so that His name remains above reproach, and no accusation can stand against Him. God is always just, always true, always faithful, a sure foundation worthy of all our trust. And when He moves by grace, the Law of God frees Him to do so. It is the Law of God that Scriptures call the love of God, the Law of God's love. John identifies that Law of God's love as this:

1 John 4:7-19 (emphasis added): *⁷Beloved, let us love one another, for love is of God, and everyone who loves has been born of God, and knows God. ⁸The one who does not love has not known God. For God is love. ⁹In this the love of God was revealed in us, because God sent His only begotten Son into the world that we might live through Him. ¹⁰***In this is love, not that we loved God, but that He loved us and sent His Son to be the propitiation concerning our sins.****¹¹Beloved, if God so loved us, we ought also to love one another. ¹²No one has seen God at any time.* ***If we love one another, God dwells in us, and His love is perfected in us.*** *¹³By this we know that we dwell in Him, and He in us, because He has given us of His Spirit.¹⁴And we have seen and testify that the Father sent the Son to be the Savior of the world. ¹⁵***Whoever shall confess that Jesus is the Son of God, God dwells in him and he in God.*** *¹⁶And we have known and believed the love that God has in us.* ***God is love, and he who abides in love abides in God, and God in him.****¹⁷In this is our love made perfect, that we may have boldness in the day of judgment, that as He is, so also we are in this world. ¹⁸There is no fear in love, but perfect love casts out fear, because fear has torment. He who fears has not been perfected in love.* ***¹⁹We love Him because He first loved us.*** *(MKJV)*

God set in motion a plan He conceived before time began. A plan not based in need but a desire to express and receive love. From this plan God built into creation a great mystery concealed within the marriage covenant He established between man and woman. In this covenant the two become one flesh, each completing the other. In this covenant they would share their lives together, and reproduce in order to pass on something of themselves. God did this demonstrating His intentions to enter into a marriage covenant with a woman. The woman would be a new creation, made from God Himself and therefore compatible and complimentary to God. Through this union He would father offspring to share the inheritance He set aside before the world began. God accomplished all this through the birth, life, death and resurrection of Christ.

PART 2: THE FULFILLMENT OF MARRIAGE

CHAPTER 4 Jesus Christ—the Hope of Israel

In Proverbs 13:12 Solomon writes," *Hope deferred makes the heart sick, But when the desire comes, it is a tree of life."* (*NKJV*) The constant putting off of the anticipated, expected or promised only makes heart-sick those looking for the object of hope. However, once realized or made tangible, the object of hope actually brings life to the seeker, just like the tree in the Garden of Eden. As Christians we know the Tree of Life symbolically spoke of Christ's work in the earth.

John 3:16-17 says, "For God so loved the world that He gave His only begotten Son, that whoever believes in Him should not perish but have everlasting life. For God did not send His Son into the world to condemn the world, but that the world through Him might be saved." (*NKJV*)

Referring to Himself, Jesus stated His purpose in coming to Israel:

Matthew 15:24: and he answering said, "I was not sent except to the lost sheep of the house of Israel." (Young's Literal Translation)

And again in Matthew 5:

Matthew 5:17-19: [17]Think not that I came to destroy the law or the prophets: I came not to destroy, but to fulfil. [18]For verily I say unto you, till heaven and earth pass away, one jot or one tittle shall in no wise pass away from the law, till all things be accomplished. [19]Whosoever therefore shall break one of these least commandments, and shall teach men so, shall be called least in the kingdom of heaven: but whosoever shall do and teach them, he shall be called great in the kingdom of heaven." (American Standard Version)

Matthew 5:17-19 (also Luke 24:44-47) coupled with Proverbs 13:12 contains the key to understanding the role of Christ and the completeness of His work.

Matthew 5:17: Do not think that I came to destroy the Law or the Prophets. I did not come to destroy but to fulfill, and Proverbs 13:12: Hope deferred makes the heart sick, but when a desire is fulfilled, it brings a tree of life.

Who is the tree of life? Christ. That's more than just a romantic notion; it is prophecy foretelling that when the tree of life came, He would fulfill the hope and the promises made to Israel. The Word of God (John 1: 1-14) made the promises and Christ fulfilled those promises... to Israel. We must understand that the Israel of the Old Covenant received the promises. God imbedded these promises in the Mosaic Law (ceremonial law), the Prophetic writings, the Psalms and even Israel's ancient history. Paul summed up the promises and also stated the foundational reason that God named Old Covenant Israel His people:

*Romans 9:1-5 (emphasis added): [1]I tell the truth in Christ, I do not lie, my conscience also bearing me witness in the Holy Spirit, [2]that I have great heaviness and continual pain in my heart. [3]For I myself was wishing to be accursed from Christ for my brothers, my kinsmen according to the flesh, [4]who are Israelites; to whom belong the **adoption**, and the **glory**, and the **covenants**, and the **giving of the Law**, and the **service of God**, and the **promises**; [5]whose are the fathers, and **of whom is the Christ according to flesh**, He being God over all, blessed forever. Amen. (MKJV)*

In Matthew 15:24 Jesus said, *"...I was not sent except to the lost sheep of the house of Israel."* It was the people of Israel who received the covenants, and it was the people of Israel who were promised Messiah (Shiloh, Son of David) would come from them, and through them bring salvation to the world. So in order for salvation to come to the world, it had to first come to Israel, correct? That's what Paul says in Romans chapters 8-11. Although chapter 8 may seem to stand apart from the other three chapters, it actually sets the tone for the whole section. I will not give place here for an exhaustive study of chapter 8, however let me point out some phrases for you to consider. (Words are drawn from the *New King James Version*.)

Israel as the object of God's affection
- Called according to God's purpose—8:28
- Foreknew by God—8:29
- God's elect—8:33
- God did not forsake Israel nor would be separated from Her during her great trouble—8:33-37
- Inseparable from God's love—8:39

God gave Israel preeminence
- First fruits of the Spirit—8:23
- Predestined, called, justified, glorified—8:29
- Christ, the firstborn of many—8:29

God's purpose for Israel
- To redeem the body of Israel—8:23-25
- Intercession for the saints to God through the Spirit—8:26-27
- Predestined to be conformed to the image of Christ—8:29
- To endure many hardships to bring forth Christ—8:33-36

God's salvation to all nations through Israel
- Condemnation of the Law ended by condemning sin in the flesh of Jesus Christ—8:1-4

- Freedom to please God by being spiritually minded— 8:5-9
- Resurrection life—8:9-11
- Sons and heirs—8:14-19
- Freely give all things through Christ—8:32

Romans chapters 9-11:
- Paul's love and concern for his people—9:1-2; 10:1, 11:1-5, 11
- Israel of the flesh (older, Ishmael, Esau, Pharaoh, Law,) versus Israel of the promise (younger, Isaac, Jacob, Moses, faith)—9:4-33; 10:2-21
- God's dealing with both branches lead Israel to salvation, accomplishes God's promises, and brings God eternal glory. 11:6-10, 12-36
  1. Natural branches—Unbelieving, disobedient Israel
  2. Holy branches—Obedient/Remnant Israel, believing Gentiles

Romans 8:35-39: [35]Who shall separate us from the love of Christ? Shall tribulation or distress, or persecution, or famine, or nakedness, or peril, or sword? [36]As it is written: "For Your sake we are killed all day long; We are accounted as sheep for the slaughter." [37]Yet in all these things we are more than conquerors through Him who loved us, [38]For I am persuaded that neither death nor life, nor angels, nor principalities nor powers, nor things present nor things to come, [39]nor height nor depth, nor any other created thing, shall be able to separate us from the love of God which is in Christ Jesus our Lord. (NKJV)

God bound Himself to Israel through covenant. Nothing could separate her from that love.

Going to Romans 9, Paul uses the promise in Old Testament prophesy to show God's intention for all people:

> *Romans 9:22-26: [22]What if God, wanting to show His wrath and make His power known, endured with much longsuffering the vessels of wrath prepared for destruction, [23]and that He might make known the riches of His glory on the vessels of mercy, which He had prepared beforehand for glory, [24]even us whom He called, not of the Jews only, but also of the Gentiles? [25]As He says also in Hosea: "I will call them My people, who were not My people, and her beloved, who was not beloved." [26]And it shall come to pass in the place where it was said to them, "You are not My people," There they shall be called sons of the living God. (NKJV)*

God made a promise of marriage to a people, and He called that people Israel. Was Israel born Israel? No, Israel was born Jacob; God changed his name to Israel. In previous chapters I presented that God created this enormous universe yet remained alone in it. God desired a mate suitable for Himself and began a process by which He created for Himself a mate. So we have this love story, the foundation of all great love stories. This story begins with God wanting to share Himself with a wife, and looking throughout creation, He sees a galaxy. Searching throughout that galaxy He sees a planet. God chooses this planet to bring forth a unique creation. God then chooses a man, and says to that man, "From your seed shall all peoples of the earth be blessed." God then establishes a covenant with this man Abraham to bring forth a nation with an earthly and spiritual destiny. This nation He calls Israel, purposed to come from His own body, a mate created for God Almighty. Through their union children would be born to receive a great inheritance worthy of God's name, power and authority.

CHAPTER 5   The Marriage of God to Israel

As Christians, we understand God's dealing with Old Covenant Israel through their history. How Jacob, who God renamed "Israel," moved his whole family to Egypt by the grace of God manifested through Joseph. God blessed them there until the Egyptians enslaved them. God then delivered them from bondage by the hand of Moses who performed great wonders before Pharaoh, prompting him to release the children of Israel. Moses led them from Egypt, through the wilderness, and to the land God promised to give to the seed of Abraham. On the way to their inheritance God made a covenant with the people of Israel through Moses as the mediator. Regarding His intentions God said:

> Exodus 6:6-8: *"⁶Therefore say to the children of Israel: "I am the Lord; I will bring you out from under the burdens of the Egyptians, I will rescue you from their bondage, and I will redeem you with an outstretched arm and with great judgments. ⁷I will take you as My people, and I will be your God. Then you shall know that I am the Lord your God who brings you out from under the burdens of the Egyptians. ⁸And I will bring you into the land which I swore to give to Abraham, Isaac, and Jacob; and I will give it to you as a heritage: I am the Lord." (NKJV)*

God made a marriage covenant with the people of Israel just as He promised to Abraham, Isaac, and Jacob. On Mt. Sinai God gave Israel the terms of the marriage covenant:

> Exodus 19:4-8: *⁴You have seen what I did to the Egyptians, and I bore you on eagles' wings and brought you to Myself. ⁵And now if you will obey My voice indeed, and keep My covenant, then you shall be a peculiar treasure to Me above all the nations; for all the earth is Mine. ⁶And you shall be to*

Me a kingdom of priests and a holy nation. These are the words which you shall speak to the sons of Israel.⁷And Moses came and called for the elders of the people, and laid before their faces all these words which Jehovah commanded him. ⁸And all the people answered together and said, All that Jehovah has spoken we will do. And Moses returned the words of the people to Jehovah. (MKJV)

The discourse between the people of Israel and God mediated through Moses demonstrates the covenantal foundation of their marriage. God fulfills the promise of His love by bringing Israel out of bondage to another nation, He loved them first. He then offers the terms of the marriage covenant to Israel with the ongoing promise of bringing them into the land of their promises, which they accept. Moses betrothed Israel to God. I say betrothed because God's promises still remained unfulfilled; until the terms of the marriage covenant reach fulfillment then the marriage cannot happen. What terms remain unfulfilled? Reread Exodus 6:6-8 above, and note how God says he gives the land as a heritage.

God gave Israel two terms He obligated Himself to fulfill:

1. God promised to rescue them from Egypt.
2. God promised to bring them into the land promised to their forefathers Abraham, Isaac and Jacob.
    - Abraham: Gen. 12:6-7, Gen. 13:14-17
    - Isaac: Gen. 26:1-6, 24
    - Jacob: Gen. 28:3-4, Gen. 35:9-13

God fulfilled the first part that He made to the children of Israel, yet the promise made to the Fathers remained unfulfilled until Israel came into their land of promise. God, as the initiator of the marriage, had to fulfill the terms He promised to the Fathers or else the marriage covenant stood nullified.

Israel also had terms to meet:

1. Circumcision: Gen. 17:-14
2. Obey the terms of the covenant: Ex. 19:5

Obviously, the weight of marriage rested much greater upon the shoulders of God. However, God not only fulfilled His terms, He exceeded them. The testimony of His fulfillment came from the witness of Israel itself:

Joshua 23:4-5 (emphasis added): ***⁴****Behold, I have divided to you by lot these nations that are left to be an inheritance for your tribes, from Jordan, with all the nations that I have cut off, even to the Great Sea westward.* ***⁵And Jehovah your God shall put them out from before you, and drive them out of your sight. And you shall possess their land, as Jehovah your God has promised to you.*** *(MKJV)*

Joshua 24:8-18: (emphasis added) *⁸And I brought you into the land of the Amorites who lived on the other side of the Jordan. And they fought with you, and **I gave them into your hand so that you might possess their land.** And I destroyed them from before you.* *⁹Then Balak the son of Zippor, king of Moab, arose and warred against Israel, and sent and called Balaam the son of Beor to curse you.* *¹⁰But I would not listen to Balaam. And he still blessed you. And I delivered you out of his hand.* *¹¹And you went over Jordan and came to Jericho. And the men of Jericho fought against you, the Amorites, and the Perizzites, and the Canaanites, and the Hittites, and the Girgashites, the Hivites, and the Jebusites. And **I delivered them into your hand.*** *¹²And I sent the hornet before you, **which drove them out from before you**, the two kings of the Amorites, not with your sword, nor with your bow.* ***¹³And I have given you a land for which you did not labor, and cities which you did not build, and you live in them. You now eat of the vineyards and olive-yards which you did not plant.*** *¹⁴Now therefore, fear the Lord, serve Him in* *sincerity and in truth, and put away the gods which your fathers served on the other side of the River and in Egypt. Serve the Lord. ¹⁵And if it seems evil to you to serve Jehovah, choose this day whom you will serve, whether the gods which your fathers served Beyond the River, or the gods of the Amorites in whose land you live. But as for me and my house, we will serve Jehovah. ¹⁶And the people answered and said, "Far be it from us to forsake Jehovah to serve other gods. ¹⁷For Jehovah our God is He who brought us and our fathers up out of the land of Egypt, from the house of bondage. And He did those great wonders in our sight, and kept us in all our way in which we went and among all the people through whom we passed. ¹⁸And **Jehovah drove out from before us all the people**, even the Amorites who lived in the land. We will also serve Jehovah, for **He is our God."** (MKJV)*

Judges 2:6: (emphasis added) ⁶Now when Joshua had sent the people away, the children of Israel went every man unto his inheritance to possess the land. (ASV)

In both the Old and New Testaments are recorded other witnesses to God fulfilling His land promises to Israel.— Nehemiah 9:22-25; 1 Kings 4:20-21 (Solomon's kingdom exceeded the land promised to Israel); Acts 7:44-46, Acts 13:16-19.

Having taken possession of her inheritance by her own confession, Israel professes the God of Abraham, Isaac and Jacob as her God and the marriage covenant comes into full effect. God accomplished His word to Israel by bringing her out of Egypt. God then brought her into Canaan, driving out its inhabitants and giving Israel possession of their land as her inheritance. Israel must then continue to keep her terms of the covenant through circumcision and following the ceremonial Law given through Moses. God and Israel were married.

To the people of Israel, the taking of the land meant more than just obtaining real estate; and coming into their inheritance meant more than acquiring wealth. The terms of the covenant stated in Exodus chapters 6 and 19 confirmed that all the earth belonged to God and to show that Israel held a special place among the nations, he gave Canaan to them to take possession of as an inheritance. For Israel to be in their land meant that they continued to hold a special place with God above all other nations. As long as they remained in their land they remained married to God.

CHAPTER 6   The Unfaithful Wife

Unfaithfulness to God characterized the nation of Israel toward her husband. Israel had no king because God ruled over them and He gave them judges to lead them. When the people worshipped the gods of other nations, God disciplined Israel by giving them over to oppression by these other nations. God then raised up judges to deliver the people and turn them back to their God. Then Israel committed a great sin against her husband when she lusted after the other nations, demanding a king to rule over her. This account is recorded in 1 Samuel 8:

> *1Samuel 8:4-7: (emphasis added) ⁴ Then all the elders of Israel gathered themselves together, and came to Samuel unto Ramah;⁵ and they said unto him, Behold, thou art old, and thy sons walk not in thy ways: now make us a king to judge us* **like all the nations**.*⁶ But the thing displeased Samuel, when they said, Give us a king to judge us. And Samuel prayed unto Jehovah.⁷ And Jehovah said unto Samuel, Hearken unto the voice of the people in all that they say unto thee; **for they have not rejected thee, but they have rejected me, that I should not be king over them.** (ASV)*

So Israel increased in her unfaithfulness until the reign of Solomon's son Rehoboam when the ten northern tribes of Israel cut themselves off from their inheritance in God, leaving the southern two tribes as God's people. Both houses of Israel over hundreds of years were drawn away to other gods and made alliances with other nations for security. The northern kingdom of Israel rebelled immediately and degenerated much faster, while the southern kingdom of Judah eventually fell into deeper levels of depravity than the north. Calling all Israel an adulterous people, God condemns and judges both houses for forsaking their marriage vows.

Marriage must first be defined as the covenantal relationship between God and His people. Because of marital unfaithfulness, the people of Israel risked losing their relationship with God and be cut off from their inheritance. Ezekiel chapter 16 provides the basis of God's charge against all Israel:

> *Ezekiel 16:1-6: ¹Again the word of the Lord came to me, saying,² "Son of man, cause Jerusalem to know her abominations,³ and say, ' Thus says the Lord God of Jerusalem: "your birth and your nativity are from the land of Canaan; your father was an Amorite and your mother a Hittite.⁴ As for your nativity, on the day you were born your navel cord was not cut, nor were you washed in water to cleanse you; you were not rubbed with salt or wrapped in swaddling cloths.⁵ No eye pitied you, to do any of these things for you, to have compassion on you; but you were thrown out into the open field, when you yourself were loathed on the day you were born.⁶ And when I passed by you and saw you struggling in your own blood, I said to you in your blood, 'Live!' Yes, I said to you in your blood, 'Live!'" (NKJV)*

God reminds the people of Israel that they were not always the people of God. God found Israel despised and discarded among the nations. Israel existed without hope or future until God saw her and showed compassion toward her.

> *Ezekiel 16:7-8: ⁷I made you thrive like a plant in the field; and you grew matured, and became very beautiful. Your breasts were formed, your hair grew, but you were naked and bare. ⁸When I passed by you again and looked upon you, indeed your time was the time of love; so I spread My wing over you and covered your nakedness. yes, I swore an oath to you and entered into a covenant with you, and you became Mine, says the Lord God. (NKJV)*

The ongoing narrative occurring here in Ezekiel depicts the compassion and love of God toward those despised by the rest of the world. God not only brings life to Israel but patiently waits for her to come of age that He may show favor through the marriage covenant. He comes to her after she has reached maturity, seeing her naked and uncovered. No one married her so she remained uncovered until God saw her. Ezekiel prophesied that God spread His wing over her demonstrating His intentions to marry her.

> Ezekiel 16:9-14: *⁹Then I washed you in water; yes, I thoroughly washed off your blood, and I anointed you with oil.¹⁰ I clothed you in embroidered cloth and gave you sandals of badger skin; I clothed you with fine linen and covered you with silk.¹¹ I adorned you with ornaments, put bracelets on your wrists, and a chain on your neck.¹² And I put a jewel in your nose, earrings in your ears, and a beautiful crown on your head.¹³ Thus you were adorned with gold and silver, and your clothing was of fine linen, silk, and embroidered cloth. You ate pastry of fine flour, honey, and oil. You were exceedingly beautiful, and succeeded to royalty.¹⁴ Your fame went out among the nations because of your beauty, for it was perfect through My splendor which I had bestowed on you, says the Lord God. (NKJV)*

God demonstrated great love and affection toward Israel even covering her in His splendor. However, something was wrong. This object of God's affection practiced her own form of affection that brought offense to her husband.

> Ezekiel 16:15: *¹⁵But you trusted in your own beauty, played the harlot because of your fame, and poured out your harlotry on everyone passing by who would have it. (NKJV)*

Ezekiel goes on prophesying that the beautiful things God gave Israel which made her so distinctive and famed, Israel used to commit adultery with other gods and nations. Her adultery reaches such depths of perversion that God says in Ezekiel 16:

> *Ezekiel 16:32-34: ³² You are an adulterous wife, who takes strangers instead of her husband. ³³ " Men make payment to all harlots, but you made your payments to all your lovers, and hired them to come to you from all around for your harlotry. ³⁴ "You are the opposite of other women in your harlotry, because no one solicited you to be a harlot. In that you gave payment but no payment was given you, therefore you are the opposite." (NKJV)*

God's accusation against His wife states, "You are worse than a harlot because you did not accept payment; you actually paid lovers to commit adultery against me." So what happened? Why did things go so wrong? This account seems to expose a flaw in God's plan. God finds a wife in Israel yet under the first marriage covenant she demonstrates great unfaithfulness. Could such a thing be true? Why did God build a marriage on a law that His wife would not keep? How could God have designed such utter failure?

Remember that marriage first describes God's intentions toward mankind. God works to make for Himself a wife from His own body to be suitable to Himself. God worked to make for Himself a wife. So if God's intended design from the beginning focused on making for Himself a wife, then the covenant on which that marriage stood must also contribute to making a wife suitable for God. Therefore the Mosaic Law's purpose was to reveal the unfaithful heart of Israel toward God, not the failure of God's wisdom or plan.

> *Deuteronomy 31:16-21: (emphasis added) ¹⁶And Jehovah said to Moses, "Behold, you shall sleep with your fathers. And this people shall rise up and go lusting after the gods of the strangers of the land into which they are going, into their*

midst. And they will forsake Me and break My covenant which I made with them. ¹⁷ Then My anger shall be kindled against them in that day, and I will forsake them. And I will hide My face from them, and they shall be devoured, and many evils and troubles shall befall them, so that they will say in that day, Have not these evils come on us because our God is not among us? ¹⁸ And I will surely hide My face in that day for all the evils which they have done, for **they shall turn to other gods.** *¹⁹ Now, therefore, write this song for you, and teach it to the sons of Israel. Put it in their mouths, so that this song may be a witness for Me against the sons of Israel. ²⁰ For when I shall have brought them into the land which I swore to their fathers, the land that flows with milk and honey, and they shall have eaten and have become satisfied, and become fat, then* **turn to other gods and serve them, and provoke Me and break My covenant.** *²¹ And it shall be when many evils and troubles have found them, this song shall testify against them as a witness. For it shall not be forgotten out of the mouths of their seed.* **For I know their imagination which they do, even now, before I have brought them into the land which I swore." (MKJV)**

Joshua 24:19-24: ¹⁹ And Joshua said to the people, "You cannot serve Jehovah, for He is a holy God. He is a jealous God. He will not forgive your transgressions nor your sins. ²⁰ If you forsake Jehovah and serve strange gods, then He will turn and do you harm, and destroy you after He has done you good." ²¹And the people said to Joshua, "No, but we will serve Jehovah." ²² And Joshua said to the people, "You are witnesses against yourselves that you have chosen Jehovah, to serve Him." And they said, "We are witnesses."²³ "And now put away the strange gods among you, and incline your heart to Jehovah, the God of Israel."²⁴ And the people said to Joshua, "We will serve Jehovah our God, and His voice we will obey." (MKJV)

Isaiah 29:13-14 (Matthew 15:7-9): [13] *And the Lord said, "Forasmuch as this people draw nigh unto me, and with their mouth and with their lips to honor me, but have removed their heart far from me, and their fear of me is a commandment of men which hath been taught them;* [14]*therefore, behold, I will proceed to do a marvelous work among this people, even a marvellous work and a wonder; and the wisdom of their wise men shall perish, and the understanding of their prudent men shall be hid." (ASV)*

Acts 7:37-41: (emphasis added) [37]*This is that Moses who said to the sons of Israel, "The Lord your God shall raise up a Prophet to you from your brothers, One like me; you shall hear Him."* [38] *This is he who was in the congregation in the wilderness with the Angel who spoke to him in Mount Sinai, and with our fathers, who received the living words to give to us,*[39] *to whom our fathers would not be obedient, but thrust him away and* **turned back again to Egypt in their hearts,**[40] *saying to Aaron,* **"Make us gods to go before us,** *for as for this Moses who brought us out of the land of Egypt, we do not know what has become of him."*[41] **And they made a calf in those days and offered sacrifice to the idol and rejoiced in the work of their own hands**. *(MKJV)*

God's righteousness demands a righteous wife comparable to Himself, so her heart must be exposed by the light of God's law. God committed Himself to the process necessary to obtain a wife. His love made Him subject to the continual betrayal and contempt of a people that worshiped Him in His presence, while looking for opportunity to indulge their perversions. This thread weaves all through scripture. Israel practiced harlotry because she possessed the heart of a harlot from the beginning.

CHAPTER 7   God—the Betrayed Husband

We know through the history of the Old Testament that all Israel (northern and southern kingdoms) offended God to the point that He removed them from the land. Because of the sin of Solomon, God removed the ten northern tribes from their heritage.

> *1Kings 11:9-13: (emphasis added) ⁹And Jehovah was angry with Solomon because his heart was turned from Jehovah, the God of Israel, who had appeared to him twice¹⁰ and had commanded him concerning this thing, that he should not go after other gods; and he did not keep that which Jehovah commanded.¹¹ And Jehovah said to Solomon, "Since this is done by you, and since you have not kept My covenant and My statutes which I have commanded you, I will surely tear the kingdom from you and will give it to your servant.¹² But I will not do it in your days, for David your father's sake, but I will tear it out of the hand of your son.¹³ Only, I will not tear away all the kingdom, **but I will give one tribe to your son for David My servant's sake, and for Jerusalem's sake which I have chosen.**" (MKJV)*

However, in order to bring Israel into a future of life and peace, God established a covenant with the House of David separate from the Mosaic Covenant. This covenant promised to send the Messiah to restore all things concerning Israel. (2 Sam. 7:12-16, 23:5; 1 Chron. 28:2). Based on this Davidic Covenant, Judah (the tribe of David) had to be preserved as the remnant of Israel.

The northern kingdom God kicked out first starting with Jeroboams rebellion in 1Kings 12.

1Kings 12:15-20: ¹⁵ *And the king did not listen to the people, for the cause was from Jehovah, that He might perform His saying which Jehovah spoke by Ahijah of Shiloh to Jeroboam the son of Nebat.*¹⁶ *And all Israel saw that the king did not listen to them, and the people answered the king, saying, What part do we have in David? Yea, there is no inheritance in the son of Jesse. To your tents, O Israel! Now see to your house, O David! And Israel went to its tents.*¹⁷ *As for the sons of Israel, those living in the cities of Judah, Rehoboam reigned over them.*¹⁸ *And King Rehoboam sent Adoram, who was over the tribute. And all Israel stoned him with stones so that he died. And King Rehoboam made haste to go up to get into a chariot to flee to Jerusalem.*¹⁹ *And Israel rebelled against the house of David to this day.*²⁰ *And it happened when all Israel heard that Jeroboam had come again, they sent and called him to the company, and made him king over all Israel. There was none who followed the house of David, but the tribe of Judah only.* (MKJV)

Once the northern kingdom of Israel cut herself off from the heritage God provided, she quickly debased herself into all forms of adultery and perversion until God judged her:

Jeremiah 3:6-8: (emphasis added) ⁶ *Moreover Jehovah said unto me in the days of Josiah the king, Hast thou seen that which backsliding Israel hath done? she is gone up upon every high mountain and under every green tree, and there hath played the harlot.* ⁷ *And I said after she had done all these things, She will return unto me; but she returned not: and her treacherous sister Judah saw it.*⁸ *And I saw, when, for this very cause that backsliding Israel had committed adultery,* **I had put her away and given her a bill of divorcement,** *yet treacherous Judah her sister feared not; but she also went and played the harlot.* (ASV)

So complete was the judgment against Israel that God declared the north would *"never rise up again"* (Amos 8:14-<u>MKJV</u>). At the close of the history of the northern kingdom Assyria conquered and dispersed her throughout the nations, divorced and cast out by her husband.

The southern kingdom which consisted of the tribes of Judah and Benjamin did remain true to God for a little while, but eventually she also forsook her husband. In contrast to the north, Judah became worse than Israel yet because of God's covenant with David, God did not divorce her.

> *1Kings 11:30-33: ³⁰And Ahijah caught hold of the new robe on him, and tore it in twelve pieces.³¹ And he said to Jeroboam, Take ten pieces for yourself. For so says Jehovah, the God of Israel, "Behold, I will tear the kingdom out of the hand of Solomon and will give ten tribes to you, ³² but he shall have one tribe for My servant David's sake, and for Jerusalem's sake, the city which I have chosen out of all the tribes of Israel,³³ because they have forsaken Me, and have worshiped Ashtoreth the goddess of the Sidonians, Chemosh the god of the Moabites, and Milcom the goddess of the sons of Ammon, and have not walked in My ways, to do what is right in My eyes, and to keep My statutes and My judgments, as David his father did." (MKJV)*

> *Jeremiah 3:7-10: ⁷ And I said after she had done all these things, Turn to Me! But she did not return. And her treacherous sister Judah saw it.⁸ And I saw, when for all the causes for which backsliding Israel committed adultery, I sent her away and gave a bill of divorce to her, yet her treacherous sister Judah did not fear, but she went and whored, she also. ⁹And it happened, from the folly of her whoredom, she defiled the land and fornicated with stones and stocks. ¹⁰ And yet for all this her treacherous sister Judah has not turned to Me with her whole heart, but with falsehood, says Jehovah. (MKJV)*

God did cast out Judah for a period of 70 years to give the land rest, however He promised to return them to their land to serve Him again.

> Jeremiah 29:10-14: *¹⁰For so says Jehovah, When according to My Word seventy years have been fulfilled for Babylon, I will visit you and confirm My good Word to you, to bring you back to this place.¹¹ For I know the purposes which I am purposing for you, says Jehovah; purposes of peace and not of evil, to give you a future and a hope.¹² Then you shall call on Me, and you shall go and pray to Me, and I will listen to you. ¹³ And you shall seek Me and find Me, when you search for Me with all your heart. ¹⁴ And I will be found by you, says Jehovah; and I will turn away your captivity, and I will gather you from all the nations, and from all the places where I have driven you, says Jehovah. And I will bring you again into the place from where I caused you to be exiled. (MKJV)*

God restored Jerusalem to Judah and the exiles but they did not maintain possession of their inheritance, they now served under the lordship of other nations. Apostle Paul refers to the nations in Galatians 4:1-5 as "governors, tutors, guardians and stewards," purposed as overseers of God's people until Messiah came. In this time of subjection, the people reminded themselves of the promise of God to remarry them; not just Judah but the whole of Israel. This hope again rests in the revealing of the Messiah that would fulfill all things. The prophets spoke often of the restoration of Israel to God.

> Isaiah 53:1-6: *¹Who hath believed our message? and to whom hath the arm of Jehovah been revealed?² For he grew up before him as a tender plant, and as a root out of a dry ground: he hath no form nor comeliness; and when we see him, there is no beauty that we should desire him.³ He was despised, and rejected of men; a man of sorrows, and acquainted with grief: and as one from whom men hide their*

face he was despised; and we esteemed him not.⁴ Surely he hath borne our griefs, and carried our sorrows; yet we did esteem him stricken, smitten of God, and afflicted.⁵ But he was wounded for our transgressions, he was bruised for our iniquities; the chastisement of our peace was upon him; and with his stripes we are healed.⁶ All we like sheep have gone astray; we have turned every one to his own way; and Jehovah hath laid on him the iniquity of us all. (ASV)

*Ezekiel 36:22-28: (emphasis added) ²²Therefore say unto the house of Israel, Thus saith the Lord Jehovah: I do not this for your sake, O house of Israel, but for my holy name, which ye have profaned among the nations, whither ye went.²³ And I will sanctify my great name, which hath been profaned among the nations, which ye have profaned in the midst of them; and the nations shall know that I am Jehovah, saith the Lord Jehovah, when I shall be sanctified in you before their eyes.²⁴ For I will take you from among the nations, and gather you out of all the countries, and will bring you into your own land.²⁵ And I will sprinkle clean water upon you, and ye shall be clean: from all your filthiness, and from all your idols, will I cleanse you.²⁶ **A new heart also will I give you, and a new spirit will I put within you; and I will take away the stony heart out of your flesh, and I will give you a heart of flesh.**²⁷ And I will put my Spirit within you, and cause you to walk in my statutes, and ye shall keep mine ordinances, and do them.²⁸ And ye shall dwell in the land that I gave to your fathers; **and ye shall be my people, and I will be your God.** (ASV)*

Jeremiah 31:31-34: (emphasis added) ³¹Behold, the days come, saith Jehovah, that I will make a new covenant with the house of Israel, and with the house of Judah: ³² not according to the covenant that I made with their fathers in the day that I took them by the hand to bring them out of the land of Egypt; which my covenant they brake, although I was a *husband unto them, saith Jehovah.*³³ *But this is the covenant that I will make with the house of Israel after those days, saith Jehovah: I will put my law in their inward parts, and in their heart will I write it;* **and I will be their God, and they shall be my people:**³⁴ *and they shall teach no more every man his neighbor, and every man his brother, saying, Know Jehovah; for they shall all know me, from the least of them unto the greatest of them, saith Jehovah:* **for I will forgive their iniquity, and their sin will I remember no more.** (ASV)

Jeremiah 32:37-40: (emphasis added) ³⁷ *Behold, I will gather them out of all the countries, whither I have driven them in mine anger, and in my wrath, and in great indignation; and I will bring them again unto this place, and I will cause them to dwell safely:*³⁸ *and they shall be my people, and I will be their God:*³⁹ *and I will give them one heart and one way, that they may fear me forever, for the good of them, and of their children after them:*⁴⁰ **and I will make an everlasting covenant with them, that I will not turn away from following them, to do them good; and I will put my fear in their hearts, that they may not depart from me.** (ASV)

God set His heart and mind on a course to make for Himself a wife. He married Israel under a covenant that exposed the harlotry in her stony heart and the lack of love she truly held for her husband.

God chose all of Israel but preserved Judah and the House of David to redeem a people for Himself. Both Israel and Judah broke the covenant and suffered for it; yet, God determined to make a wife for Himself. He promised to keep a remnant until He made a new marriage covenant with them through Messiah.

CHAPTER 8   God Divorces Israel

When dealing with the issue of marriage in the church, the issue of divorce always lurks in the shadow of our minds. In Part 3, "The Administration of Marriage," I will deal more in-depth with the subject of divorce among Christians. In this chapter the focus continues with the dominant theme of God making for Himself a wife. God chose Israel to be His special people, His love, His wife. Though He was a husband to her and elevated her above all nations, she demonstrated continual unfaithfulness to the Marriage Covenant and to her husband's love. The Marriage Covenant mediated through Moses (referred to as the Mosaic Covenant) exposed the adulterous heart of Israel. Because of Israel's adulterous heart God divorced His wife:

> Jeremiah 3:8-11: *8And I saw, when, for this very cause that backsliding Israel had committed adultery, I had put her away and given her a bill of divorcement, yet treacherous Judah her sister feared not; but she also went and played the harlot. 9 And it came to pass through the lightness of her whoredom, that the land was polluted, and she committed adultery with stones and with stocks.10 And yet for all this her treacherous sister Judah hath not returned unto me with her whole heart, but feignedly, saith Jehovah. 11 And Jehovah said unto me, Backsliding Israel hath showed herself more righteous than treacherous Judah." (ASV)*

Christ deals with the issue of divorce with the Pharisees:

> Mark 10:2-12: *2 And tempting Him, the Pharisees came to Him and asked Him, Is it lawful for a man to put away his wife?3 And He answered and said to them, 'What did Moses command you?'4 And they said, 'Moses allowed a bill of divorce to be written, and to put her away.' 5 And Jesus*

answered and said to them, 'He wrote you this precept because of the hardness of your hearts. ⁶ But from the beginning of the creation God made them male and female. ⁷For this cause a man shall leave his father and mother and shall cleave to his wife. ⁸ And the two of them shall be one flesh. So then they are no longer two, but one flesh. ⁹Therefore what God has joined together, let not man put apart.' ¹⁰ And in the house His disciples asked Him again about the same.¹¹ And He said to them, 'Whoever shall put away his wife and marries another commits adultery against her. ¹² And if a woman shall put away her husband and marries to another, she commits adultery.'" (MKJV)

In this account (also in Matt. 19), the Pharisees tempt Jesus by asking a trick question, "Is it lawful for a man to put away his wife." The trick in this question implies that the Law has anything to say regarding "putting away." For a man to put away his wife meant to simply kick her out of his house; no divorce. This practice commonly occurred in Judea after the return of the exiles from Babylon. What made this action so evil is that it used the Law as a manipulation tool against Godly wives. Since no divorce occurred, the regulations concerning marriage still held sway over the wife. She could not remarry or else she suffered the condemnation of the Law regarding adultery. Property and inheritance passed on through the men, so to be "put away" meant living with no means of support. Because of the outcry by wives against their treacherous husbands, God accuses the men of Judah of corrupting the covenant of their fathers through abusing their covenant wives:

Malachi 2:13-16: ¹³ And this is a second thing you have done, covering the altar of Jehovah with tears, weeping, and groaning, yet not facing toward the food offering, and taking it with delight from your hand. ¹⁴ Yet you say, Why? Because Jehovah has been witness between you and the wife of your youth, against whom you have dealt treacherously; yet she is your companion and your covenant wife. ¹⁵ And did He not make you one? Yet the vestige of the Spirit is in him. And what of the one? He was seeking a godly seed. Then guard your spirit, and do not act treacherously with the wife of your youth. ¹⁶ Jehovah, the God of Israel, says He hates sending away; and to cover with violence on his garment, says Jehovah of Hosts. Then guard your spirit, and do not act treacherously." (MKJV)

As stated before, God's giving of the Law meant to reveal the corrupt hearts of His people. By pressing the question, "What did Moses command you?" Jesus not only revealed the perverse heart of the Pharisees, He also revealed the intent of God as husband. The Pharisees respond to Jesus with the truth and therefore the condemnation of their perversion, "Moses allowed a bill of divorce to be written, and to put her away." Jesus then reveals the truth of the Law, "He wrote you this precept because of the hardness of your hearts." God knew that unless he demanded the men of Israel actually free their wives through a bill of divorce, then they could oppress them without regard. The bill of divorce also gave the men of Israel the protection to legally "cut off" an unfaithful wife, and thus protect name, inheritance and assets.

How did the Law regarding divorce reveal the intent of God as husband to Israel? It allowed God to show love to His wife by freeing her to marry another. God was making for Himself a wife, however, the Law revealed her heart to be treacherous, adulterous and cold toward her husband. Knowing this, God provided a way that freed her to pursue another lover so that when He redeemed her, she would respond out of love and desire for Him. The book of Hosea provides the clearest example of God's love on this matter. God told the prophet Hosea to marry a wife of adultery and love her as God loves

Israel. In unfaithfulness she left him but God tells Hosea to redeem her and love her again:

Hosea 2:2-3: (emphasis added) ² *Contend! Contend with your mother, for **she is not my wife, nor am I her husband**. Let her therefore put away her fornications out of her sight, and her adulteries from between her breasts,* ³ *lest I strip her naked and set her out as in the day that she was born; and lest I make her as the wilderness, and set her like a dry land, and slay her with thirst.(MKJV)*

Hosea 2:6-10: ⁶ *Therefore behold, I will hedge your way with thorns, and wall up her wall, that she shall not find her paths.* ⁷ *And she shall follow after her lovers, but she shall not overtake them. She shall seek them, but shall not find them. Then she shall say, I will go and return to my first husband, for then it was better with me than now.* ⁸ *For she did not know that I gave her grain, and wine, and oil, and multiplied her silver and gold, which they prepared for Baal.* ⁹ *So I will return and take away My grain in its time, and my wine in its season, and will recover my wool and my flax given to cover her nakedness.* ¹⁰ *And now I will uncover her shamefulness in the sight of her lovers, and none shall deliver her out of my hand.(MKJV)*

Hosea 2:13-20: (emphasis added) ¹³ *And I will visit on her the days of the Baals, in which she burned incense to them, and she adorned herself with her nose-rings and her jewels, and* ***she went after her lovers and forgot Me, says Jehovah.*** ¹⁴*Therefore, behold, I will lure her and bring her into the wilderness, and speak comfortably to her.* ¹⁵ *And I will give her vineyards to her from there, and the valley of Achor for a door of hope. And she shall sing there, as in the days of her youth, and as in the day when she came up out of the land of Egypt.* ¹⁶ *And it shall be at that day, says Jehovah, you shall call Me, My Husband, and shall no more call Me, My Baal.* ¹⁷ *For I will* *take away the names of the Baals out of her mouth, and **they will no more be remembered by their name.** [18] And in that day I will cut a covenant for them, with the beasts of the field, and with the birds of the heavens, and with the creeping things of the ground. And I will break the bow and the sword and the battle out of the earth, and will make them to lie down safely. [19] And I will betroth you to Me forever. Yea, I will betroth you to Me in righteousness, and in judgment, and in loving-kindness, and in mercies. [20] I will even betroth you to Me in faithfulness. And you shall know Jehovah." (MKJV)*

*Hosea 3:1-5: (emphasis added) [1] And Jehovah said unto me, Go again, love a woman beloved of her friend, and an adulteress, **even as Jehovah loveth the children of Israel, though they turn unto other gods,** and love cakes of raisins. [2] So I bought her to me for fifteen pieces of silver, and a homer of barley, and a half-homer of barley; [3] and I said unto her, Thou shalt abide for me many days; thou shalt not play the harlot, and thou shalt not be any man's wife: so will I also be toward thee.[4] For the children of Israel shall abide many days without king, and without prince, and without sacrifice, and without pillar, and without ephod or teraphim: [5] afterward shall the children of Israel return, and seek Jehovah their God, and David their king, and shall come with fear unto Jehovah and to his goodness in the latter days." (ASV)*

Returning to Mark 10, God repeats the purpose for marriage-- His marriage:

Mark 10:6-9: [6] But from the beginning of the creation God made them male and female. [7] For this cause a man shall leave his father and mother and shall cleave to his wife. [8] And the two of them shall be one flesh. So then they are no longer two, but one flesh. [9] Therefore what God has joined together, let not man put apart. (MKJV)

This is an incredibly powerful statement. The statement starts at creation, Christ restates it and Paul restates it again in Ephesians 5:31. God took one, made in His image. God then took from the one flesh and bone, and made two. God then brought her to him and the two again became one. God created out of His own flesh and bone a wife for Himself. The flesh and bone of Christ made possible the joining of God to Israel. Marriage is about God and His wife; God made for Himself a wife.

The Pharisees and Jews did not understand. Their corrupt and perverse minds held little value for marriage. To them the principals of marriage and divorce only served as instruments of manipulation or obstacles to overcome. Therefore, their attempts to trap Jesus utterly failed because they failed to understand the Law of God's love. The Pharisees only understood Law, Christ personified God's love. The Pharisees perceived marriage as Law, "This is what the Law says. How can we get around it?" However, Jesus taught, "I'm not talking to you about the Law. I'm talking to you about Myself." God was betrayed, God's wife was unfaithful to Him. Jesus' role restored marriage to God by the death of His flesh and bone, initiating a New Marriage Covenant. The purpose of the Old Covenant Law was to point to Christ, not something to be manipulated and twisted to authorize or justify a course of behavior. As we read in Ephesians 5:32, the story of God and Old Covenant Israel remained the great mystery until revealed through Christ's marriage to New Covenant Israel which He renamed the Church. Israel betrayed God; she committed adultery against Him; she polluted the land with whoredom; she took His love and traded it to lovers for favors. Despite the pathetic attempts of the Pharisees to dispute the Law, Jesus stayed focused on His purpose to fulfill the Law, and through fulfillment redeem the house of Israel from the curse of the Law, marrying her again.

In the subject of divorce God divorced Himself from unfaithful Israel, but through Messiah, paid the price for her redemption, remarrying her by a new covenant. Once again, Jesus refers to Himself, not man. Marriage first declares God's love and intentions toward mankind. Separating marriage from God shows contempt for His love, for redemption, for salvation, for eternal life, the hope of resurrection, of everything good and beautiful. Therefore when the Lord Jesus says, "What God has joined together let no man separate...," the weight of God's intentions for marriage established since before creation rests on His command. Marriage belongs to God, don't touch it.

CHAPTER 9   God's Plan to Remarry Israel

The promise of God to remarry Israel sounds great, yet the Law of Moses forbids remarrying a wife who has given herself to another.

> *Deuteronomy 24:1-4:* [1] *When a man has taken a wife and married her, and it happens that she finds no favor in his eyes, because he has found some uncleanness in her, then let him write her a bill of divorce and put it in her hand, and send her out of his house.* [2] *And when she has departed from his house, she goes and becomes another man's;* [3] *and the latter husband hates her and writes her a bill of divorce and puts it in her hand and sends her out of his house; or if the latter husband dies, he who took her to be his wife* [4] *her former husband, who sent her away, may not take her again to be his wife after she is defiled. For that is hateful before Jehovah. And you shall not cause the land to sin, which Jehovah your God gives you for an inheritance. (MKJV)*

God prophesies this law through Jeremiah to communicate His intentions to Israel: "[1]*They say, 'If a man divorces his wife, and she goes from him and becomes another man's, may he return to her again?' Would not that land be greatly polluted? But you have played the harlot with many lovers; Yet return to me,"* says the Lord.—Jer. 3:1" (NKJV) The old Mosaic Law stated that if a husband finds uncleanness with his wife he may divorce her. The husband must provide her, in her hand, a written divorce. Then he sends her out of his house. She may find another husband, but if that husband does the same thing, and provides her a certificate of divorce in her hand, or if he passes away, the first husband cannot take her back as a wife. The Law says that she stands "defiled." The term "defiled" only refers to her first husband. For him to take her back as his wife pollutes the land, a sign of the abomination committed against their inheritance in God. Here in Jeremiah we see the foundation of not only the Mosaic Covenant but also the New Covenant established through Jesus; love. God's love for Israel and Judah overcomes His wrath and desire for judgment. God makes for Himself a wife, submitting Himself to the consequences of His endeavor. God continually pleaded with His wife to return to Him.

In the book of Hosea, God directed the prophet to perform arguably the most difficult act of obedience of all His holy prophets. He commands Hosea to redeem his unfaithful wife and bring her back into his home and love her again. They would not engage in conjugal relations until an appointed time when Hosea remarried her (Hosea 3). Hosea's action prophesied God's intention; however, God's intention could not be carried out under the Mosaic Law. God would remarry Israel under a new covenant-- but how? In Hebrews 8 the writer says,

> *Hebrews 8:1-7: (emphasis added)* *[1]Now this is the main point of the things we are saying: We have such a High Priest, who is seated at the right hand of the throne of the Majesty in the heavens, [2] a Minister of the sanctuary and of the true tabernacle which the Lord erected, and not man.[3] For every high priest is appointed to offer both gifts and sacrifices. Therefore it is necessary that this One also have something to offer.[4] For if He were on earth, He would not be a priest, since there are priests who offer the gifts according to the law; [5]**who serve the copy and shadow of the heavenly things**, as Moses was divinely instructed when he was about to make the tabernacle..." What happened under the Old Covenant served as a shadow or symbol of something more infinite and substantial that was going to come. "... For He said, 'See that you make all **things according to the pattern shown you on the mountain.'**[6] But now He has obtained a more excellent ministry, inasmuch as He is also Mediator of a better*

covenant, which was established on better promises.[7] **For if that first covenant had been faultless, then no place would have been sought for a second."** *(NKJV)*

God's design for the first covenant mediated by Moses only functioned temporarily. He intended for the first covenant to end. Why, because the first covenant patterned better things to come. The first marriage covenant that God established with Israel shadowed the great intentionality of His love toward all mankind. Paul ties together the prophetic work of both Moses and Hosea in his letter to the Romans.

> *Romans 9:14-26: (emphasis added)* [14] *What shall we say then? Is there not unrighteousness with God? Let it not be!* [15]*For He said to Moses, "I will have mercy on whom I will have mercy, and I will have compassion on whom I will have compassion."* [16] **So then it is not of the one willing, nor of the one running, but of God, the One showing mercy.** [17]*For the Scripture says to Pharaoh, "Even for this same purpose I have raised you up, that I might show My power in you, and that My name might be declared throughout all the earth."* [18]*Therefore He has mercy on whom He will have mercy, and whom He will, He hardens.* [19] *You will then say to me, Why does He yet find fault? For who has resisted His will?* [20] *No, but, O man, who are you who replies against God? Shall the thing formed say to Him who formed it, Why have you made me this way?* [21] *Does not the potter have power over the clay, from the same lump to make one vessel to honor and another to dishonor?* [22] *What if God, willing to show His wrath and to make His power known, endured with much long-suffering the vessels of wrath fitted to destruction;*[23] *and that He might make known the riches of His glory on the vessels of mercy which He had before prepared to glory;* [24] *whom He also called, not only us, of Jews, but also of the nations?* [25] *As He also says in Hosea, "I will call those not My people, My people; and those not beloved, Beloved."* [26] *And it shall be, in the place*

where it was said to them. "You are not My people; there they shall be called sons of the living God." (MKJV)

Let's go back to Hebrews 8:8-10: *[8] Because finding fault with them," (those under the Old Covenant), "He says: "Behold, the days are coming, says the Lord, when I will make a new covenant with the house of Israel and with the house of Judah--[9] "not according to the covenant that I made with their fathers in the day when I took them by the hand to lead them out of the land of Egypt; because they did not continue in My covenant, and I disregarded them, says the Lord.[10] "For this is the covenant that I will make with the house of Israel after those days, says the Lord: I will put My laws in their mind and write them on their hearts; and I will be their God, and they shall be My people." (NKJV)*

Please understand that only through external or ceremonial compliance could the Mosaic Law be kept. The Old Covenant never addressed the heart. God appealed to Israel to love Him through keeping the Mosaic Law but they could keep the Law and still sin in their hearts. Hebrews 8 exposes this weakness in the Mosaic Law. God found fault with them because the Law exposed their stony, adulterous hearts.

Going to Isaiah, Jesus sums up His accusation against the Jews with the statement, *"[7]Hypocrites! Well did Isaiah prophesy about you, saying: [8]'These people draw near to Me with their mouth, And honor Me with their lips, [9]And in vain they worship Me, Teaching as doctrines the commandments of men'"* (Matt 15:7-9, Is. 29:13--*NKJV*) The Jews of Jesus' day actually did keep the Law and then some, however their hearts still wanted to hide from God by keeping external commandments and traditions. They revealed the true nature of their hearts by not recognizing their Messiah and instead wanted to kill Him. They kept the covenant to whatever extent they kept it, but their hearts were never after God. So when God says, "I will make a new covenant" it had to be a covenant of love. The Old Covenant took the form of an arranged marriage:

> *Exodus 6:6-8: (emphasis added)* [6] *Wherefore say unto the children of Israel,' I am Jehovah, and* **I will bring you out** *from under the burdens of the Egyptians, and* **I will rid you** *out of their bondage, and* **I will redeem you** *with an outstretched arm, and with great judgments:*[7] *and* **I will take you** *to me for a people, and* **I will be to you a God**; *and ye shall know that I am Jehovah your God, who bringeth you out from under the burdens of the Egyptians.*[8] *And* **I will bring you** *in unto the land which I sware to give to Abraham, to Isaac, and to Jacob; and* **I will give it you for a heritage**: *I am Jehovah.'" (ASV)*

However, the New Covenant requires the people to want to be married to God. He would not go to a people again and take them and say, "You are mine." Greater expectation rests on those that come under the New Covenant; however, greater promises come with the New Covenant. God's demonstration of love demands a response of love in return; then God embraces them and marries them. That was the promise of Hebrews 8:11: "[11]None of them shall teach his neighbor, and none his brother, saying, 'Know the Lord,' for all shall know Me, from the least of them to the greatest of them" (NKJV) How could they know him, because they love Him. No formula to follow, no list of duties to perform, no sacrifices to be made, no special observances, only love.

> *1John 4:7-19: (emphasis added)* [7] *Beloved, let us love one another: for love is of God; and every one that loveth is begotten of God, and knoweth God.* [8] *He that loveth not knoweth not God; for God is love.* [9] *Herein was the love of God manifested in us, that God hath sent his only begotten Son into the world that we might live through him.* [10] *Herein is love, not that we loved God, but that he loved us, and sent his*

Son to be the propitiation for our sins. **11 Beloved, if God so loved us, we also ought to love one another. 12 No man hath beheld God at any time: if we love one another, God abideth in us, and his love is perfected in us:** 13 *hereby we know that we abide in him and he in us, because he hath given us of his Spirit.* 14 *And we have beheld and bear witness that the Father hath sent the Son to be the Saviour of the world.* **15 Whosoever shall confess that Jesus is the Son of God, God abideth in him, and he in God.** 16 *And we know and have believed the love which God hath in us. God is love; and he that abideth in love abideth in God, and God abideth in him.* 17 *Herein is love made perfect with us, that we may have boldness in the day of judgment; because as he is, even so are we in this world.* 18 *There is no fear in love: but perfect love casteth out fear, because fear hath punishment; and he that feareth is not made perfect in love.*19 **We love, because he first loved us.** *(ASV)*

He loved us first, but if we love Him in return, then He will make His abode with us, and us with Him. God established intimacy in marriage; intimacy between God and His people. How must this love be expressed? I respond through my individual acceptance and adherence to the New Covenant established through the blood of the Christ, Jesus of Nazareth.

CHAPTER 10   Restored Virginity and New Name

Throughout this section I explain that God takes Israel from point A, the adulterous wife with a stony heart toward her husband; to point B, the faithful wife with a heart of love toward her husband. Where point A starts with a marriage covenant based on weaker promises designed to reveal the unfaithful heart of Israel; point B ends with a new marriage covenant based on greater promises revealing the mutual love between God and His people. The next question I address is how? How can God just end one Law and start with another? If He is Holy and Just, how can the switching of covenants not be seen as random or unjust by those that accuse Him? In order to preserve His great name God must change covenants in such a way that He stands above reproach and justified when judging those that choose to remain under the Old Covenant. The Mosaic Law forbids a husband to remarry his former wife yet God promises to do it. We know that through the scriptures God promises to remarry Israel under a New Covenant, yet there must be a legal process for that to occur or else God stands accused of breaking His own Law and therefore polluting the land.

Remember the Law of Moses demands that when a husband divorces his wife and she marries another man, and either through divorce or death she becomes available, he cannot marry her again. She remains defiled to him. Yet God promises to do just that; Isaiah 62 gives the legal process for God's remarriage.

Isaiah 62:1-5: (emphasis added) ¹For Zion's sake I will not hold My peace, And for Jerusalem's sake I will not rest, Until her righteousness goes forth as brightness, And her salvation as a lamp that burns. ²The Gentiles shall see your righteousness, and all the kings your glory. **You shall be called by a new name, which the mouth of the Lord will name.**³ *You shall also be a crown of glory in the hand of the Lord, and a royal diadem in the hand of your God.⁴ You shall no longer be termed Forsaken, nor shall your land any more be termed Desolate; But you shall be called Hephzibah (my delight), and your land Beulah (married); For the Lord delights in you, and your land shall be married.* **⁵For as a young man marries a virgin, so shall your sons marry you; and as the bridegroom rejoices over the bride, so shall your God rejoice over you.**" *(NKJV)*

In Isaiah 62, God promises not to keep silent ("hold my peace") or rest until He restores Jerusalem to her place of glory and honor. She would dazzle the nations once again but through her righteousness and salvation, the glory of her husband's hand. The Old Testament scriptures richly overflow with this terminology; however Isaiah prophesies something new, God's two-fold plan to accomplish his promise:

- *"You shall be called by a new name, which the mouth of the Lord will name"*-vs 2
- *"For as a young man marries a virgin, so shall your sons marry you, and as the bridegroom rejoices over the bride, so shall your God rejoice over you."*-vs 5

In order to remarry His wife God would do two things—change her name and restore her virginity, both accomplished through the New Covenant.

"You shall be called by a new name, which the mouth of the Lord will name." God established precedent with the Patriarchs when changing a name in covenantal context:

- Abram to Abraham—Gen. 17:1-5
- Sarai to Sarah—Gen. 17:15-16
- Isaac named by God—Gen.17:18-19

- Jacob to Israel—Gen. 32:22-30

Each time God changed a name He declared the name to the recipient. The name change not only carried prophetic meaning but it literally transformed the individual's nature and position. When God sent Moses to the children of Israel in Egypt, He invoked the names He gave to the Patriarchs.

Exodus 6:6-8: ⁶ Therefore say to the sons of Israel, I am Jehovah, and I will bring you out from under the burdens of the Egyptians, and I will rescue you out of their bondage. And I will redeem you with a stretched-out arm, and with great judgments. ⁷ And I will take you to Me for a people, and I will be to you a God. And you shall know that I am Jehovah your God, who brings you out from under the burdens of the Egyptians. ⁸ And I will bring you in to the land concerning which I lifted up My hand to give it to Abraham, to Isaac, and to Jacob. And I will give it to you for a heritage. I am Jehovah! (MKJV)

At Mt. Sinai, God again brought to remembrance Jacob's name, the covenant name, and His promise of love:

Exodus 19:2-6: ² And they journeyed from Rephidim, and came to the desert of Sinai, and had pitched in the wilderness. And Israel camped there in front of the mount. ³ And Moses went up to God, and Jehovah called to him out of the mountain, saying, You shall say to the house of Jacob, and tell the sons of Israel: ⁴ You have seen what I did to the Egyptians, and I bore you on eagles' wings and brought you to Myself. ⁵And now if you will obey My voice indeed, and keep My covenant, then you shall be a peculiar treasure to Me above all the nations; for all the earth is Mine. ⁶ And you shall be to Me a kingdom of priests and a holy nation. These are the words which you shall speak to the sons of Israel. (MKJV)

Remember that according to Hebrews 1:1-2 and 8:5-6, the Old Covenant shadowed the reality and substance of the New Covenant. So where does the name change occur in the New Covenant?

> Matthew 16:13-19: (emphasis added) *¹³When Jesus came into the region of Caesarea Philippi, He asked His disciples saying,* **'Who do men say that I, the Son of Man, am?'** *¹⁴So they said, 'Some say John the Baptist, some Elijah, and others Jeremiah or one of the prophets.' ¹⁵He said to them,* **'But who do you say that I am?'** *¹⁶Simon Peter answered and said,* **'You are the Christ, the Son of the living God.'** *¹⁷Jesus answered and said to him, 'Blessed are you Simon Bar-Jonah, for flesh and blood has not revealed this to you,* **but My Father who is in heaven.** *¹⁸'And I also say to you that* **"you are Peter, and on this rock I will build my church, and the gates of Hades shall not prevail against it.** *¹⁹"And I will give you the keys of the kingdom of heaven, and whatever you bind on earth will be bound in heaven, and whatever you loose on earth will be loosed in heaven." (NKJV)*

In Matthews account and also in Mark 8:27-29, we find the fulfillment of Exodus chapters 6 and 19 as well as Isaiah 62:2, "*...You shall be called by a new name, which the mouth of the Lord will name.*"

Matthew 16:13-19 reveals the fulfillment of Mt. Sinai as Jesus brings to remembrance the Old Covenant name, the New Covenant name, and God's promise of love:

- *Who do men say that I, the Son of Man, am?*—Old Covenant name for Messiah.
- *You are the Christ, the Son of the living God.*—New Covenant name for Messiah.
- *...flesh and blood has not revealed this to you, but My Father who is in heaven.*—the mouth of the Lord spoke it through Simon.

- *...you are Peter, and on this rock I will build my church, and the gates of Hades shall not prevail against it.--* Simon's name change to Peter in accordance to covenantal context.
- *And I will give you the keys of the kingdom of heaven, and whatever you bind on earth will be bound in heaven, and whatever you loose on earth will be loosed in heaven.*—The promise of restored glory before God.

Notice that Israel's name did not change but God's name did. Since God's name changed then His wife under the New Covenant would carry a new name reflecting her greater status (My church).

God also promised to restore Israel's virginity, so how does the New Covenant accomplish that? First of all I hope you can see through God's dealings with Israel, that God does not define virginity as something biological but in terms of sexual purity. Israel lost her virginity because of her fornication and adultery during her time of betrothal and marriage to her husband. Israel sinned against her husband and her vows to Him. Yet in Isaiah, her husband promises to restore her virginity to her. The only way to restore her virginity is to remove the offense or sin. Since God stands as the offended husband, only He can remove it, however the Law demands a penalty. Someone must pay the price of redemption and Israel could not redeem herself without being destroyed. God promised to restore her not destroy her. Therefore, only God could pay the price for His wife's redemption. Why would God do such a thing, because God loved His wife. Israel's redemption rests solely in the love and intent of God to forgive her adultery by removing her sin. God through His Christ fulfilled the demands of the Old Covenant marriage while at the same time establishing a New Covenant marriage, Hebrews 10 explains this process:

*Hebrews 10:1-7: (emphasis added) ¹For the law having a shadow of the good things to come, and not the very image of the things, can never with these same sacrifices, which they offer continually year by year, make those who approach perfect. ²For then would they not have ceased to be offered? For the worshippers once purified, would have had no more consciousness of sins. ³**But in those sacrifices there is a reminder of sins every year. ⁴For it is not possible that the blood of bulls and of goats could take away sins.** ⁵Therefore, when He came into the world, He said, "Sacrifice and offering You did not desire, but **a body You have prepared for Me.** ⁶In burnt offerings and sacrifices for sin You had no pleasure. ⁷Then I said, 'Behold, I have come--**in the volume of the book it is written of Me-- to do Your will, O God.** '"(NKJV)*

The writer continues in verse 12:

*Hebrews 10:12-18: (emphasis added) ¹²But this Man, after He had offered one sacrifice for sins forever, sat down at the right hand of God, ¹³From that time waiting till His enemies are made His footstool. ¹⁴**For by one offering He has perfected forever those who are being sanctified.** ¹⁵But the Holy Spirit also witnesses to us; for after He had said before, ¹⁶'This is the covenant that I will make with them after those days, says the Lord: **I will put My laws into their hearts, and in their minds will I write them.'** ¹⁷then He adds, 'Their sins and their lawless deeds I will remember no more.' ¹⁸**Now where there is remission of these, there is no longer an offering for sin."** (NKJV)*

Verse 22 gives the fulfillment of the restoration of Israel's virginity to her husband: *let us draw near with a true heart in full assurance of faith, having our hearts sprinkled from an evil conscience, and our bodies washed with pure water. (NKJV)*

If God, through Christ, takes upon Himself the penalty of
Israel's sin; and Israel, out of an act of love, accepts His
sacrifice; then her sin is paid for and removed. She no longer
bears the shame of her adultery for God's sacrifice restores her
virginity. Therefore, the true virgin wife must be those that
accept the sacrifice of Christ. Only through the New Marriage
Covenant can true Israel be reconciled and remarried to her
husband. Only through the New Marriage Covenant does God
provide for His wife Israel reconciliation and a new, better
name.

CHAPTER 11   Gentiles and the New Marriage Covenant

Up to this point I have written almost exclusively about Israel, yet anyone today would be hard-pressed to find Christians of Israelite lineage. As followers of the Lord Jesus Christ, Christians today lay hold of the promise of God's kingdom spoken over Old Covenant Israel. We embrace New Covenant terms like redemption, reconciliation, eternal life, bride of Christ, sons of God, born of the Spirit, etc. However, when gentiles sought out Jesus, He hesitated:

> *Matthew 15:22-28: (emphasis added)* ²² *And behold, a woman of Canaan coming out of these borders cried to Him, saying, Have mercy on me, O Lord, Son of David! My daughter is grievously vexed with a demon.* ²³ *But He did not answer her a word. And His disciples came and begged Him, saying, Send her away, for she cries after us.* ²⁴ *But He answered and said,* ***I am not sent except to the lost sheep of the house of Israel.*** ²⁵ *Then she came and worshiped Him, saying, Lord, help me!* ²⁶ *But He answered and said,* ***It is not good to take the children's bread and to throw it to dogs.*** ²⁷ *And she said, True, O Lord; but even the little dogs eat of the crumbs which fall from their masters' tables.* ²⁸ *Then Jesus answered and said to her, O woman,* ***great is your faith!*** *So be it to you even as you wish. And her daughter was healed from that very hour. (MKJV)*

A similar event occurred with a Roman centurion in Matthew 8:5-13 (Luke 7:2-10). These gentile "dogs" knew they stood undeserving of the Messiah's concern and unworthy to take part in Israel's promises. Jesus confirmed their status before the Jews when He said, "*...I am not sent except to the lost sheep of the house of Israel.,*" yet He acted on their behalf anyway. Why? Jesus did not act out of compassion. He did not act out of anger against the Pharisees. He did not act out of impatience with His disciples. What moved Jesus to act on the behalf of these gentiles? Only the faith of these individuals compelled Jesus to act, and not only act but use as an example to rebuke all Israel. Faith stood as the constant foundational qualifier to enter into God's favor for both the Old and New Covenants:

> Genesis15:5-6: (emphasis added) *⁵Then He brought him (Abraham) outside and said, 'Look now toward heaven, and count the stars if you are able to number them.' And He said to him, 'so shall your descendants be.' ⁶And **he believed in the Lord, and He accounted it to him for righteousness."** (NKJV)*

> *Habakkuk 2:4: Behold the proud, His soul is not upright in him; But the just shall live by his faith. (NKJV)*

> *Galatians 3:1-7: ¹O foolish Galatians! Who has bewitched you that you should not obey the truth, before whose eyes Jesus Christ was clearly portrayed among you as crucified? ²This only I want to learn from you: Did you receive the Spirit by the works of the law, or by the hearing of faith? ³Are you so foolish? Having begun in the Spirit, are you now being made perfect by the flesh? ⁴Have you suffered so many things in vain—if indeed it was in vain? ⁵Therefore He who supplies the Spirit to you and works miracles among you, does He do it by the works of the law, or by the hearing of faith?—⁶just as Abraham 'believed God, and it was accounted to him for righteousness.' ⁷Therefore know that only those who are of faith are sons of Abraham. (NKJV)*

> *Hebrews 11:1-2—"¹Now faith is the substance of things hoped for, the evidence of things not seen. ²For by it the elders obtained a good testimony." (NKJV)*

If the key to righteousness and pleasing God rests with faith, then why did Jesus hesitate regarding the Canaanite woman and Roman centurion? Why did Jesus say He was only sent to the lost sheep of Israel? How do the gentiles share in the marriage of God to Israel? Paul addresses this question in Romans chapter 9:

> Romans 9:1-5: *¹I tell the truth in Christ, I do not lie, my conscience also bearing me witness in the Holy Spirit, ² that I have great heaviness and continual pain in my heart. ³ For I myself was wishing to be accursed from Christ for my brothers, my kinsmen according to the flesh, ⁴ who are Israelites; to whom belong the adoption, and the glory, and the covenants, and the giving of the Law, and the service of God, and the promises; ⁵ whose are the fathers, and of whom is the Christ according to flesh, He being God over all, blessed forever. Amen. (MKJV)*

Paul reaffirms in Romans the preeminence of Israel "according to the flesh" and that Israel's heritage secured for them the first option to enter into the New Covenant. Christ appeared first to the house of Israel because the promises declared it. When preaching, Jesus went to the synagogues first to present the kingdom of God before preaching to the masses. Likewise, the Apostles preached in the synagogues first before engaging the gentiles. However when those in the synagogue rejected the message, the obligation to Israel after the flesh stood fulfilled and no longer binding. The message of the Messiah coming in the flesh to Israel according to the flesh was the greatest of all the promises. By rejecting their Messiah they disqualify themselves from the promises and open the way for the gentiles to hear and enter the Kingdom. Paul teaches again in Romans chapters 9-11 that God fulfilled His promise to Israel through the obedience of the remnant, that is, the few that heard and believed. Remember that the early church consisted of the house of Israel exclusively until the salvation of the house of Cornelius in Acts 10. When speaking of the remnant (a theme common among the prophets), Isaiah prophesied this:

> *2Kings 19:30-31 (Isaiah 37:31-32):* ³⁰ *And the remnant that has escaped of the house of Judah shall yet again take root downward and bear fruit upward.* ³¹ *For out of Jerusalem shall go forth a remnant, and they who escape out of Mount Zion. The zeal of Jehovah of Hosts shall do this." (MKJV)*

Finally, Moses prophesied in Deuteronomy 18:18-19 (Acts 3:22-23, 7:37): (emphasis added)

> ¹⁸*I will raise up for them a Prophet like you from among their brethren, and will put My words in His mouth, and He shall speak to them all that I command Him.* ¹⁹***And it shall be that whoever will not hear My words, which He speaks in My name, I will require it of him." (NKJV)***

Paul's concerns for Israel after the flesh came out of His understanding of the Law, Prophets and Psalms which Messiah would fulfill. Israel's rejection of Messiah fulfilled the Law and Prophets. The grafting in of the gentiles into the promises of Israel also fulfilled the Law and Prophets as the Apostles testified in Acts 15:1-20. Specifically, the Apostle James quotes the prophet Amos:

> *Amos 9:11-12:* ¹¹ *In that day will I raise up the tabernacle of David (house or dynasty of David) that is fallen, and close up the breaches thereof; and I will raise up its ruins, and I will build it as in the days of old;* ¹² *that they may possess the remnant of Edom, and all the nations that are called by my name, saith Jehovah that doeth this. (ASV)*

Isaiah again prophesies:

> *Isaiah 49:5-6: (emphasis added)* ⁵ *And now, says Jehovah who formed Me from the womb to be His servant, to bring Jacob*

*again to Him, Though Israel is not gathered, yet I shall be glorious in the eyes of Jehovah, and My God shall be My strength. ⁶ And He said, It is but a little thing that You should be My servant to raise up the tribes of Jacob, and to bring back the preserved ones of Israel; **I will also give You for a light to the nations, to be My salvation to the end of the earth.**" (MKJV)*

Returning back to Matthew 5, Jesus said this:

*Matthew 5:17-20: (emphasis added) ¹⁷ Think not that I came to destroy the law or the prophets: I came not to destroy, but **to fulfil.** ¹⁸ For verily I say unto you, Till heaven and earth pass away, one jot or one tittle shall in no wise pass away from the law, **till all things be accomplished.** ¹⁹ Whosoever therefore shall break one of these least commandments, and shall teach men so, shall be called least in the kingdom of heaven: but whosoever shall do and teach them, he shall be called great in the kingdom of heaven. ²⁰ For I say unto you, that except your righteousness shall exceed the righteousness of the scribes and Pharisees, ye shall in no wise enter into the kingdom of heaven. (ASV)*

Scripture teaches that the Old Covenant had an expiration date, being the fulfillment of God's promises to Israel. Once fulfilled then the Old Covenant and everything connected to it would pass away revealing the House of David restored. The restored House of David included the remnant of Israel that remained obedient to the New Covenant established under Messiah, but also the obedient from among the gentiles. Paul's concern for Israel in Romans stems from a realization that all things had not been fulfilled at the time of his writing. How does Paul know this? The Temple in Jerusalem and even all Israel, whose very existence depended upon the Old Covenant, remained intact. Therefore, Israel after the flesh had time to enter into the New Marriage Covenant established through their Messiah. The Apostles referred to this period as the "last days":

- Acts 2:16-22 (Joel 2:28-32)—Pouring out of the Holy Spirit would occur in the "last days"
- Hebrews 1:1-2— The writer acknowledges that the promises spoken through the prophets, Christ inherited in "these last days."
- James 5:1-9—James addresses the abuse of the rich over the just in his day. The ungodly rich accumulated wealth in the "last days" but it would be destroyed. James encourages the just to be patient because the Lord's coming was near, indicating the just would soon see the destruction of the wealth of the ungodly rich. *"Behold, the Judge stands before the door." (MKJV)*
- 2 Peter 3:1-4—Peter identifies the scoffers of his day as reminders to the Christians of his day that they lived in the "last days."

The last days came to their end with the destruction of Jerusalem and the Temple in 70 A.D. The end not only freed the house of Israel from the bondage of the Old Covenant, but it also identified the true Israel. In Romans 9, Paul identifies the true Israel:

> *Romans 9:6-8: 6But it is not that the word of God has taken no effect. For they are not all Israel who are of Israel, 7nor are they all children because they are the seed of Abraham; but, 'In Isaac your seed shall be called.' 8That is, those who are the children of the flesh, these are not the children of God; but the children of the promise are counted as the seed." (NKJV)*

What identifies the "seed of Abraham" and therefore the "children of promise" who are qualified to enter into the New Marriage Covenant? Paul explains again in Galatians 3:6-7-- 6just as Abraham 'believed God, and it was accounted to him for righteousness.' ⁷Therefore know that only those who are of faith are sons of Abraham. (*NKJV*)

Although Paul is the most prolific in the New Testament regarding the identity of true Israel, he only repeats what John the Baptist (Matthew 3:8-9, Luke 3:7-8)and Christ Jesus (John 8:33-40, Matthew 8:5-12) declare.

So we know that faith in God through the work of the Lord Jesus Christ qualified not only Israel to enter the New Covenant but all who believed on Him. How then would the gentiles take part in the promises of the New Marriage covenant?

- Israel after the flesh had to experience the promise of the Son of Man first; according to the prophets—Isaiah 53:6, Ezekiel 34:23, Matthew 15:24.
- God changed the name of the "Son of Man" to the "Christ"; according to the prophets—Isaiah 62:2, Matthew 16:15-19, Mark 14:61-62.
- Only the remnant of Israel would believe on the Christ and enter into the New Covenant; according to the prophets—2 Kings 19:30-31, Isaiah 1:7-9, 10:20-22, Joel 2:32.
- Christ changed remnant Israel's name to His church; according to the prophets --Isaiah 62:2, 65:13-15; Jeremiah 33:16, Matthew 16:15-19.
- The rejection of Israel after the flesh made the way clear for the Gentiles to enter in; according to the prophets— Deuteronomy 32:21, Isaiah 65:1-2, Romans 10:19-21
- Gentiles must believe on Christ, just as remnant Israel after the Spirit had done; according to the prophets— Isaiah 2:2-4, 60:1-3, Zechariah2:10-13,.8:20-23, Amos 9:9-12, Jeremiah 16:19-21, Romans 9:22-26
- The Gentiles coming into the New Covenant would make Israel after the flesh jealous; according to the

prophets—Deuteronomy 32:21, Psalms 69:22-23, Romans 11:7-15

- Jealous Israel had to enter into the New Covenant before the end of the "last days" to become remnant Israel; according to the prophets—Jeremiah 31:16-20, 31-34, Isaiah 28:16, Psalms 118:22, Isaiah 8:14, Hosea 2:19-23., 1Peter 2:6-10
- The Old Covenant reached its fulfillment; according to the prophets—Deuteronomy 32:18-29, Isaiah 10:20-23, Matthew 24:1-3 (Hebrews 9:6-8), Hebrews 8:7-13, 10:23-25 and its passing was marked by the destruction of Jerusalem and its temple in A.D.70
- With the destruction of Jerusalem and the Temple, the Old Marriage Covenant no longer existed, only the New Marriage Covenant established by Christ remained.— Hebrews 13:10-15
- God exalted true Israel when the New Marriage Covenant became fully established, according to the prophets—Isaiah 1:21-29, 61:1-9, 62:1-5, 65:13-19, Zechariah 9:9-10 (Matthew 21:5-7)

True Israel consists of those that believe like Abraham and love God through Christ from the heart—Israel and Gentile (Romans 1:16, 10:12, Galatians 3:28, Colossians 3:11). God labored to make for Himself a wife. He endured great hardship and suffering over millennia by those He loved:

> 1John 4:10—*"¹⁰In this is love, not that we loved God, but that He loved us and sent His Son to be the propitiation for our sins." (NKJV)*

Yet in spite of Israel's unfaithfulness God remained faithful: faithful to see His work completed, faithful to the promises made in His name, faithful to the one He loved to redeem her and restore her to the place of His favor. How great is the love of God.

PART 3: THE ADMINISTRATION OF MARRIAGE

CHAPTER 12   Love Demonstrated by Obedience

Jesus' obedience to the will of God was synonymous with His love for God (John 3:16). In John 10, Jesus not only affirmed this but called the Jews to judge Him accordingly:

> *John 10:24-25:* ^{24} *Then the Jews encircled Him and said to Him, How long do you make us doubt? If you are the Christ, tell us plainly.* ^{25} *Jesus answered them, I told you and you did not believe. The works that I do in My Father's name, they bear witness of Me. (MKJV)*

> *John 10:37-38:* ^{37}*If I do not do the works of My Father, do not believe Me:* ^{38} *But if I do, though you do not believe Me, believe the works so that you may know and believe that the Father is in Me, and I in Him." (MKJV)*

In Hebrews 10 Paul also affirms Jesus Christ came to fulfill God's will:

> *Hebrews 10:4-10: (emphasis added)* ^{4} *For it is not possible that the blood of bulls and of goats should take away sins.* ^{5}*Therefore when He comes into the world, He says, 'Sacrifice and offering You did not desire,* ***but You have prepared a body for Me.*** ^{6} *In burnt offerings and sacrifices for sin You have had no pleasure.* ^{7} *Then I said, Lo,* ***I come (in the volume of the Book it is written of Me) to do Your will, O God.'*** ^{8} *Above, when He said, 'Sacrifice and offering, and burnt offerings and offering for sin You did not desire, neither did You have pleasure in them' (which are offered according to the Law),* ^{9} *then He said,* ***'Lo, I come to do Your will, O God.'*** *He takes away the first so that He may establish the second.*

> ¹⁰**By this will** *we are sanctified through the offering of the body of Jesus Christ once for all. (*MKJV*)*

Why do I start this final section reminding you about Christ's obedience to the Father, because obedience to God's will determines love for God. The Apostle John records Jesus' teaching regarding love towards God being synonymous with obedience to God:

> *John 14:15: If you love Me, keep My commandments.*

> *John 14:23-24: ²³ Jesus answered and said to him, 'If a man loves Me, he will keep My Word. And My Father will love him, and We will come to him and make Our abode with him. ²⁴ He who does not love Me does not keep My Words, and the Word which you hear is not Mine, but the Father's who sent Me.'" (*MKJV*)*

Christ's commandment in John 14 reminded the Jews of God's same words spoken to them from Deuteronomy:

> *Deuteronomy 5:9-10: ⁹ You shall not bow yourself down to them, nor serve them. For I Jehovah your God am a jealous God, visiting the iniquity of the fathers upon the sons to the third and fourth generation of those who hate Me, ¹⁰ and doing mercy to thousands of those who love Me and keep My commandments. (*MKJV*)*

Once again, the scriptures return our thoughts to the foundation of marriage, love. Through Jesus' obedience to the Father's will, God demonstrated His love through a New Covenant. By our obedience to Jesus' commandments we respond in love toward God accepting His New Covenant. We therefore become part of His Church, one with Christ and the Father, who also exist as one with the Holy Spirit. Thus, God becomes one with the His Church, the object of His affection in love submitted to her Husband.

As members of Christ's Church, the body of Christ, we live as the example to the world regarding God's love. Yet, the power and simplicity of the New Covenant message suffers from the perversion of political correctness and the ineffectiveness of a weakened gospel. How can God's love be defined? Christians and non-Christians alike hear about God's love yet we seem to fall short in properly explaining it. As those called to the "ministry of reconciliation" described in 2Corinthians 5:18-19, how can Christians administer and teach God's love to the world if we struggle with its meaning.

Defining God's love requires us to first discard the populist definitions of men and false doctrines. The love of God is not tolerance. The love of God is not inclusiveness. The love of God is not seeker friendly. The love of God is not subject to our interpretation or labels. Simply put, God defines His love through His marriage Covenant:

> John 3:16-17: [16] For God so loved the world that He gave His only-begotten Son, that whoever believes in Him should not perish but have everlasting life.[17] For God did not send His Son into the world to condemn the world, but so that the world might be saved through Him. (MKJV)

God made man a special creation proving that he first loved us. However, from creation until today man continually rejects God's love. Man's rejection of God's love caused offense against Him, yet God already prepared a way that the two would be reconciled; so God chose Israel to be the vessels of His reconciliation. God covenanted with them, redeemed them, married them and suffered from their adultery and fornication. God divided them, divorced and put them away but promised to forgive and remarry them under an eternal covenant. Through this New Covenant with Israel God made possible for all men to be reconciled again to Himself. This message of reconciliation is also the message of God's love, "God laid down

His life that you might live, come be reconciled to God."
Reconciliation always takes both parties. The one party
forgives to clear the way, but the other party must respond:

> *2Corinthians 5:17-21:* [17] *So that if any one is in Christ, that
> one is a new creature; old things have passed away; behold,
> all things have become new.* [18] *And all things are of God, who
> has reconciled us to Himself through Jesus Christ, and has
> given to us the ministry of reconciliation;* [19] *whereas God was
> in Christ reconciling the world to Himself, not imputing their
> trespasses to them, and putting the word of reconciliation in
> us.* [20] *Then we are ambassadors on behalf of Christ, as God
> exhorting through us, we beseech you on behalf of Christ, be
> reconciled to God.* [21] *For He has made Him who knew no sin,
> to be sin for us, that we might become the righteousness of
> God in Him. (MKJV)*

The love of God makes possible the reconciliation between God
and man, however only by obedience to the New Covenant
does man respond in love to God. Only love through obedience
to God's Covenantal Law guarantees marriage and oneness
with God.

CHAPTER 13   Christ and the Great Mystery

In Part 1: *the meaning of marriage*, I reminded the church how God established marriage before time. That God wanted to have a wife. To communicate God's unique purpose for man the scriptures say, "In the beginning God said, 'let us make man in Our image.',", and He made one. Everything else in creation God made in multiples. But of man He said, "Let Us make man in Our image" and He made one. The singularity of man reflects the oneness of God. The importance of the oneness of God must even be acknowledged in order to follow His commandments:

> *Deuteronomy 6:4-5: [4] Hear, O, Israel. Jehovah our God is one Jehovah. [5] And you shall love Jehovah your God with all your heart and with all your soul and with all your might." (MKJV)*

Jesus confirms this commandment in the gospel of Mark:

> *Mar 12:29-30: [29] And Jesus answered him, "The first of all the commandments is, 'Hear, O Israel, the Lord our God is one Lord;[30] and you shall love the Lord your God with all your heart, and with all your soul, and with all your mind, and with all your strength.' This is the first commandment." (MKJV)*

Then God said, "It's not good that the man is alone. I will make a helpmate suitable for him." God divided man, and from the man's flesh and bone created woman and introduced her to the man. Adam confirmed Eve as "bone of my bone and flesh of my flesh" suitable to him above all creation and the two became "one flesh." Modern Christian understanding regarding marriage goes back only as far as creation which reflects our tendency as believers to see God's interaction with us egocentrically. It's all about us, or it's all about me. How many times have you heard, or even said, "If I was the only one, Christ still would have gone to the cross."; or "Christ died on the cross for me." Granted, we as individual members of the church benefit from Christ's sacrifice, but we forget that Christ died to establish a New Covenant between God and man. Through this New Covenant, God calls individuals to be reconciled to Him and be joined with Him corporately in His body, the Church. We forget God created all things for His pleasure, and our value in this covenant rests solely on God's pleasure in us. Therefore, the value of marriage rests in God not man.

When preachers, pundits, and protestors invoke the creation of Adam and Eve to strengthen their declaration, "Marriage is only between man and woman," they only weaken their position. They forget the revealing of the mystery proclaimed by the Apostle Paul in Ephesians 5:

> *Ephesians 5:31-33: (emphasis added)* [31]*For this reason a man shall leave his father and mother and be joined to his wife, and the two shall become one flesh.'* [32]*This is a great mystery, but **I speak concerning Christ and the church.*** [33]*Nevertheless let each one of you in particular so love his own wife as himself, and let the wife see that she respects her husband. (NKJV)*

Christians must recognize the creation of Adam and Eve joined as one, to be the shadow or representation of Christ the man becoming one with His wife, the church. God established marriage before time, and incorporated it into His creation as a direct reflection of His intentions toward man. He created man from the earth and woman from man; then submitted Himself to creation through Christ Jesus to create a mate suitable for Himself. The Lord Jesus Christ therefore becomes the solution to the question, the great mystery. The mystery being this-- how could God who created everything, form a mate suitable and comparable to Himself from creation? The Psalmist prophesies the coming of Messiah in Psalms 8:

Psalms 8:3-5: ³When I consider Your heavens, the work of Your fingers, The moon and the stars, which You have ordained, ⁴What is man that You are mindful of him, and the son of man that you visit him? ⁵For you have made him a little lower than the angels, And You have crowned him with glory and honor. ⁶You have made him to have dominion over the works of Your hands; You have put all things under his feet. (NKJV)

In Hebrews, Paul confirms the prophecy in Psalms 8 as being fulfilled in Christ Jesus:

Hebrews 2:6-10: (emphasis added) ⁶ But one hath somewhere testified, saying, What is man, that thou art mindful of him? Or the son of man, that thou visitest him? ⁷ Thou madest him a little lower than the angels; Thou crownedst him with glory and honor, And didst set him over the works of thy hands: **⁸Thou didst put all things in subjection under his feet.** *For in that he subjected all things unto him, he left nothing that is not subject to him. But now we see not yet all things subjected to him. ⁹* **But we behold him who hath been made a little lower than the angels, even Jesus,** *because of the suffering of death crowned with glory and honor, that by the grace of God he should taste of death for every man. ¹⁰* **For it became him, for whom are all things, and through whom are all things,** *in bringing many sons unto glory, to make the author of their salvation perfect through sufferings. (ASV)*

Through the Lord Jesus Christ, God became flesh and bone, a part of His own creation; and from His own body formed a wife for Himself, suited and comparable to Himself.

In Part 2: *the fulfillment of marriage*, we examined how God fulfilled His promise to marry Israel, how her unfaithfulness provoked God to divorce her, yet His love caused Him to promise remarriage under a New Covenant. Then at the appointed time God fulfilled His promise through the Lord Jesus Christ.

God demonstrated His intentions for mankind by choosing, and marrying a people He named "Israel." God appointed them to keep, and be the caretakers of, His Marriage Covenant. However, the people of Israel whom God called "wife" acted unfaithfully toward her husband, as proclaimed in Isaiah, Hosea and Jeremiah. In Isaiah 62 we read how God first saw Israel as a baby discarded and loved her. He cleaned her up, watched her grow and when she came of age He married her. God loved her as a husband; however Israel did not love Him in return. Israel's response to God revealed the incompleteness of the Old Covenant. The Old Covenant wasn't flawed only incomplete, by design. As Paul wrote in Romans 8:

> *Rom 8:1-4: [1] There is therefore now no condemnation to them that are in Christ Jesus. [2] For the law of the Spirit of life in Christ Jesus made me free from the law of sin and of death. [3]For what the law could not do, in that it was weak through the flesh, God, sending his own Son in the likeness of sinful flesh and for sin, condemned sin in the flesh: [4] that the ordinance of the law might be fulfilled in us, who walk not after the flesh, but after the Spirit." (ASV)*

And also in Hebrews,

> *Hebrews 10:1-3: [1] For the law having a shadow of the good things to come, not the very image of the things, can never with the same sacrifices year by year, which they offer continually, make perfect them that draw nigh. [2] Else would they not have ceased to be offered? because the worshippers, having been once cleansed, would have had no more consciousness of sins. [3] But in those sacrifices there is a remembrance made of sins year by year." (ASV)*

So God designed the Old Marriage Covenant, mediated through Moses, to accomplish two things:

- Foreshadow a better Marriage Covenant with greater promises. This foreshadowing revealed that God intended the Old Covenant to be temporary.
- Reveal the unfaithful heart of Israel to her husband and reminded her of her sin.

The Old Covenant was also an arranged marriage, "I am the God of your fathers Abraham, Isaac, and Jacob. (Exodus. 2:24, 3:15)." God arranged the terms of the marriage with the patriarchs long before Israel became a nation. The Covenant required Israel to perform dutifully, yet not out of love. Because Israel did not love God she failed to perform dutifully, which the Law of the Covenant continually reminded her.

At the height of Israel's unfaithfulness, God promised to restore her:

Isaiah 62:1-5: [1] For Zion's sake I will not be silent, and for Jerusalem's sake I will not rest, until its righteousness goes out as brightness, and her salvation as a burning lamp. [2] And the nations will see your righteousness, and all kings your glory; and you will be called by a new name, which the mouth of Jehovah will name.[3] You also will be a crown of glory in the hand of Jehovah, and a royal diadem in the hand of your God. [4] You will no more be called Forsaken; nor will your land any more be called Desolate; but you will be called My Delight is in her, and your land, Married; for Jehovah delights in you, and your land is married. [5] For as a young man marries a virgin, so will your sons marry you; and as the bridegroom rejoices over the bride, so will your God rejoice over you. (MKJV)

The love of God for His wife drove Him not to rest until He restored her reputation and virtue. He promised that when He restored her that even the nations would see her righteousness. God promised to accomplish this by giving her a new name, by restoring her virginity, and remarry her. Jesus reaffirms this promise in Matthew 16:

> *Matthew 16:13-18: (emphasis added) ¹³When Jesus came into the region of Caesarea Philippi, He asked His disciples, saying, '**Who do men say that I, the Son of Man, am**?' ¹⁴So they said. 'Some say John the Baptist, some Elijah, and others Jeremiah or one of the prophets.' ¹⁵He said to them, 'But who do you say that I am?' ¹⁶ Simon Peter answered and said, '**You are the Christ, the Son of the living God.**' ¹⁷Jesus answered and said to him, 'Blessed are you Simon Bar-Jonah, **for flesh and blood has not revealed this to you, but My Father who is in heaven.** ¹⁸And I also say to you that you are Peter, and **on this rock I will build My church**, and the gates of Hades shall not prevail against it. (NKJV)*

The title "Son of Man" identified the Messiah sent to redeem Israel and fulfill God's promises to her. God changed His name to "Christ," the new name that would identify a restored Israel, which Jesus called "My church." Jesus also changed Simon's name to Peter confirming the promised fulfillment. The new name identified the New Marriage Covenant by which God, through Christ Jesus, restored Israel's virginity. Christ remarried Israel, changing her name to the church. He also opened the gates to all men to join the New Marriage Covenant; fulfilling Isaiah 49:

> *Isaiah 49:6--Indeed He says, 'It is too small a thing that You should be My Servant To raise up the tribes of Jacob, And to restore the preserved ones of Israel; I will also give You as a light to the Gentiles, That You should be My salvation to the ends of the earth.' (NKJV)*

The Lord Jesus Christ in love fulfilled all of God's will to make for Himself a wife. Through the suffering in His flesh, Christ made a New Covenant founded in love to restore all men to God. Those who respond to His love bear the message of His reconciliation, "be reconciled to God."

CHAPTER 14   The Ministry of Reconciliation

I titled this final section "The Administration of Marriage" to remind the Church of her position before God, as the object of His affection, and her responsibility to teach and administer this New Covenant to the nations. As stated earlier in this book, without marriage there is no salvation, without marriage there is no redemption, without marriage there is no future hope, without marriage we are lost. The Old Covenant mediated by Moses and the New Covenant mediated by Christ married God to a people. God conceived both Covenants, initiated them, endured great suffering to preserve and consummate them, all to make for Himself a wife. In the end, after millennia of sacrifice, God finally joined with a wife through a Covenant of love. In this New Marriage Covenant established through the incredible suffering of His own body, God finally created a wife suitable and comparable to Himself.

In the light of God's great love for His Church, to diminish marriage in any way demonstrates a monumental level of foolishness and display of contempt for God's genius and suffering. When individual members in the body, ministers, congregations, even whole denominations stand up to redefine marriage contrary to God's definition, they set themselves up for destruction. Instead of fulfilling their obligation to educate and administer this great covenant, these members pervert marriage and reduce its importance to irrelevance. They must be reminded again of who they are and the great cost for their redemption and eternal life.

The Church does not possess exclusive rights to marriage, marriage existed from the beginning. The observance of marriage has been practiced through various forms in both pagan and God-fearing cultures from creation. God gave marriage as a gift to all men and nations, as a common thread weaved through all cultures, to draw them to Himself at the appointed time. At the revealing of His New Covenant, God commissioned His Church to administer and teach the nations its meaning; -to become one with the "Desire of all nations" foretold in Haggai 2:

> Haggai 2:6-7: [6]For thus says the Lord of hosts: 'Once more (it is a little while) I will shake heaven and earth, the sea and dry land; [7]and I will shake all nations, and they shall come to the Desire of All Nations, and I will fill this temple with glory, says the Lord of hosts. (NKJV)

Those who choose to enter the New Covenant, God appoints as ministers of reconciliation to those outside the Covenant as Paul reminds us in 2 Corinthians 5:

> 2 Corinthians 5:18-20: [18] And all things are of God, who has reconciled us to Himself through Jesus Christ, and has given to us the ministry of reconciliation; [19] whereas God was in Christ reconciling the world to Himself, not imputing their trespasses to them, and putting the word of reconciliation in us. [20] Then we are ambassadors on behalf of Christ, as God exhorting through us, we beseech you on behalf of Christ, be reconciled to God." (MKJV)

This appointment by God also makes us accountable to God for the fruit of our ministry. I am not referring to conversions or to the subject of evangelism. This book addresses the responsibility of the Church to reflect the glory of her Husband. Conversions are the result of the reconciliation of the individual heart to God by accepting the gospel of the New Covenant. God also preaches to the nations, apart from the ministry of the Church. Increasing accounts of Christians in restricted nations tell of conversions occurring outside of churches. Where the gospel message is constrained, Jesus preaches to people in dreams and visions. Even those that reject the gospel, as the Apostle Paul did, Jesus appears to them preaching reconciliation. Jesus commissioned the Church to preach the gospel (Mark 16:15) and teach the nations (Matthew 28:18-20), however only the spirit of Christ Jesus knows the heart that truly loves Him.

2 Corinthians chapter 5 teaches that Christians are ambassadors of Christ with a ministry. The ministry is a message, "be reconciled to God." As an ambassador in the world, great expectation weighs on the character and conduct of the one sent. The perception of the ambassador affects how his government is perceived, and ultimately how the message is received. If the ambassador's conduct contradicts his government's message, then he risks losing his place of authority and the message will be spoken by another. Therefore, the fruit of our ministry rests not in whether others listened and obeyed the gospel of Christ, but how we conduct ourselves as ambassadors in the performance of our ministry:

*Ephesians 4:1-6: (emphasis added) ¹ I therefore, the prisoner in the Lord, **beseech you to walk worthily of the calling wherewith ye were called**,² with all lowliness and meekness, with longsuffering, forbearing one another in love; ³ giving diligence to keep the unity of the Spirit in the bond of peace. ⁴There is one body, and one Spirit, even as also **ye were called in one hope of your calling**; ⁵ one Lord, one faith, one baptism, ⁶ one God and Father of all, who is over all, and through all, and in all." (ASV)*

*2Th 1:11-12: (emphasis added) ¹¹ To which end we also pray always for you, **that our God may count you worthy of your calling**, and fulfil every desire of goodness and every work of faith, with power; ¹² **that the name of our Lord Jesus may be glorified in you**, and ye in him, according to the grace of our God and the Lord Jesus Christ." (ASV)*

God empowered the Church to teach and administer His marriage Covenant and holds the Church accountable to fulfill its ministry. Therefore, if marriage loses its significance and meaning in the world because the Church misrepresents Christ, the Church is accountable. If a generation of people grows up dismissing marriage as cultural, and therefore a subjective observance, then the Church has poorly represented Christ and His gospel. If a people see fit to empower their government with the authority to redefine marriage, and then give that definition protection under the law, then how can the Church not share in the judgment to come upon those people? Speaking out is not enough. In America today, Christians, preachers and Christian groups fill the airwaves with protests, accusations and condemnations against every perversion in our society. Yet perversion increases while the influence of the Church in America decreases. How can this be if all that we needed to affect righteousness in our culture depended on speaking out? How can the Church lose its influence in culture when Isaiah prophesied the opposite?

> Isaiah 9:6-7: (emphasis added) [6] For unto us a child is born, unto us a son is given; and the government shall be upon his shoulder: and his name shall be called Wonderful, Counsellor, Mighty God, Everlasting Father, Prince of Peace. [7] **Of the increase of his government and of peace there shall be no end**, upon the throne of David, and upon his kingdom, to establish it, and to **uphold it with justice and with righteousness from henceforth even for ever**. The zeal of Jehovah of hosts will perform this. (ASV)

The Angel proclaimed to Mary that Jesus would fulfill this prophecy:

> Luke 1:31-33: [31] And behold, thou shalt conceive in thy womb, and bring forth a son, and shalt call his name JESUS. [32] He shall be great, and shall be called the Son of the Most High:

and the Lord God shall give unto him the throne of his father David: [33] *and **he shall reign over the house of Jacob for ever; and of his kingdom there shall be no end.** (ASV)*

To answer this question we must return to the role of an ambassador. Remember the effectiveness of the ambassador's message depends entirely on how he represents the government sending him. Again in Ephesians 4 Paul stresses the code of conduct for those called:

> *Ephesians 4:1-6* [1] *I therefore, the prisoner in the Lord, beseech you to walk worthily of the calling wherewith ye were called,* [2]*with all lowliness and meekness, with longsuffering, forbearing one another in love;* [3] *giving diligence to keep the unity of the Spirit in the bond of peace.* [4] *There is one body, and one Spirit, even as also ye were called in one hope of your calling;* [5] *one Lord, one faith, one baptism,* [6] *one God and Father of all, who is over all, and through all, and in all. (ASV)*

Christians must realize that conducting ourselves in such a way that reflects our God and Savior, permeates all areas of our lives. Our lives must reflect our confession. How do we convince the world to be reconciled to God and submit to the gospel of His eternal kingdom if it sees little difference between itself and the ambassadors sent to it? The greatest objections I personally hear for why people reject the gospel stems from accusations of hypocrisy in the Church. They see Christians acting one way on Sunday, then acting like the world the rest of the week. They have Christian friends preach the gospel to them, yet do so in a demeaning manner. They see Christians lie, cheat, and steal. They witness Christians at strip joints and getting drunk on Friday nights. They know about the adultery, fornication, and homosexuality in the Church. They see Christian business owners take advantage of their employees, even Christian employees. They see the lack of love, and they see Christians using the benefits of their faith to oppress others. Is it any wonder that our society refuses to be reconciled to God?

God designed the truth and purity of the gospel to be easily understood and accepted. But when those that should be the ambassadors of this Marriage Covenant act contrary to what the covenant demands, the world sees only hypocrisy. If the world rejects the message in spite of the faithful ambassador then they bear the consequences of their rejection. However, we must each ask the question, "Do I conduct myself in a manner that rightly reflects Christ, or does my conduct bring shame to His gospel?"

As Ambassadors of the Kingdom of God, we must address the administration of the New Covenant to the world in two areas; individually and corporately. Christianity in America places great weight on personal accountability; however, the scriptures also address the responsibility of the Church at the corporate and geographical level.

CHAPTER 15   The Law and Statutes of the New Covenant

While on Mt. Sinai, Moses received The Ten Commandments. These Commandments served as the foundation for God's Covenant with Israel:

> *Exodus 34:27-28: ²⁷ And Jehovah said to Moses, Write these words for yourself; for on the mouth of these words I have made a covenant with you and with Israel.²⁸ And he was there with Jehovah forty days and forty nights. He neither ate bread, nor drank water. And He wrote upon the tablets the words of the covenant, the Ten Commandments. (MKJV)*

God then proceeded to teach the people of Israel their responsibilities as His covenant people. These responsibilities God instructed Israel for forty years. They included observances, feasts, sacrifices, priesthood, purifying rites, ceremonial washings, the construction of the tabernacle, criminal and civil courts, giving, acceptable worship, etc. These observances were referred to as the Law of Moses, and throughout Israel's history, God blessed or punished them based on their adherence to Mosaic Law. God also made clear that Israel not only obey the Law but that God chose Her as the keeper or guardian of the Law. Hebrews chapter 10 explains the purpose for Israel to "keep" the Law:

> *Hebrews 10:4-10: (emphasis added) ⁴ **For it is not possible that the blood of bulls and of goats should take away sins.** ⁵ Therefore when He comes into the world, He says, "Sacrifice and offering You did not desire, but **You have prepared a body for Me.** ⁶ In burnt offerings and sacrifices for sin You have had no pleasure.*

*⁷ Then I said, Lo, **I come (in the volume of the Book it is written of Me) to do Your will, O God.**" ⁸ Above, when He said, "Sacrifice and offering, and burnt offerings and offering for sin You did not desire, neither did You have pleasure in them" (which are offered according to the Law), ⁹ then He said, "Lo, I come to do Your will, O God." He takes away the first so that He may establish the second. ¹⁰ **By this will we are sanctified** through the offering of the body of Jesus Christ once for all." (MKJV)*

God, through His Covenant, blessed Israel to "keep" (guard, preserve) the Law until the One promised would come. His coming marked a process of fulfilment that not only removed the burden of obeying the Mosaic Law, but also systematically lifted the responsibility of being the Law's guardian.

As Israel moved forward in history, God sent prophets to Her with signs, wonders, and warnings, reminding her of her position and responsibilities. Israel rejected and persecuted her prophets, yet God kept sending them with pleas to return to Him. During the days of David, God anointed David king and a prophet with great skill to artistically create the Psalms. In short, all of the Old Testament from Genesis to Malachi, pertains to Israel's history. The Old Testament contains Law, poetry, history, parables, teaching and prophecy. Yet Israel's history is more than history, it's also prophetic. Israel's history not only prophesied of Messiah (The Patriarchs, Joseph, Moses, Joshua, David, Boaz, Aaron, etc.), but it also prophesied of the fulfilled promises to Israel (Adam and Eve, Sarah, Isaac and Rebekah, Rahab, Boaz and Ruth, Hosea, Egypt, Babylon, etc.).

In Matthew 5, Jesus stated His purpose in coming to Israel:

Matthew 5:17-18: ¹⁷Do not think that I came to destroy the Law or the Prophets. I did not come to destroy but to fulfill. ¹⁸For assuredly, I say to you, till heaven and earth pass away, one jot or one tittle will by no means pass from the law till all is fulfilled." (NKJV)

In Luke, Jesus also included the Psalms in His role of fulfillment:

Luke 24:44: ⁴⁴Then He said to them, 'These are the words which I spoke to you while I was still with you, that all things must be fulfilled which were written in the Law of Moses and the Prophets and the Psalms concerning Me.'(NKJV)

Jesus identified the Mosaic Law, the Prophets and the Psalms as prophecy to be fulfilled through His role as The Messiah. Then Jesus made an incredible statement in Matthew 22:

Mat 22:36-40: ³⁶ Master, which is the great commandment in the Law? ³⁷ Jesus said to him, You shall love the Lord your God with all your heart, and with all your soul, and with all your mind. ³⁸ This is the first and great commandment. ³⁹ And the second is like it, You shall love your neighbor as yourself. **⁴⁰On these two commandments hang all the Law and the Prophets***. (MKJV)*

Jesus taught that loving God and loving your neighbor functioned as the foundation of the Mosaic Law and the Prophets. He emphatically reaffirms what God said when giving the Law originally:

Deuteronomy 6:4-5: ⁴Hear , O Israel: The Lord our God, the Lord is one! ⁵You shall love the Lord your God with all you heart, with all your soul, and with all your strength. (NKJV)

Leviticus 19:17-18: ¹⁷You shall not hate your brother in your heart. You shall surely rebuke your neighbor, and not bear sin because of him. ¹⁸You shall not take vengeance, nor bear any grudge against the children of your people, but you shall love your neighbor as yourself: I am the Lord. (NKJV)

By fulfilling all the Law, the Prophets, and the Psalms, Christ becomes the reality of what they signified; therefore rendering them obsolete and empty. In a very real way, Christ's revealing caused the Law, Prophets and Psalms to "pass away" leaving Christ and the 2 original commandments on which to build His New Covenant. However, the 2 commandments could not complete the New Covenant. After the Passover meal, the night before His crucifixion, Christ added a new commandment:

> *John 13:34-35:* [34] *A new commandment I give unto you, that ye love one another; even as I have loved you, that ye also love one another.* [35] *By this shall all men know that ye are my disciples, if ye have love one to another." (ASV)*

This means that under the New Covenant, all of the Law, the Prophets and the Psalms; all the history and dealings of God with Israel; all the promises God made to Israel; in essence, all the Old Covenant finds completion in Christ. Christ then reduces it all to 3 commandments:

- The Lord our God, the Lord is one! You shall love the Lord your God with all your heart, with all your soul, and with all your strength. (Submit to the gospel of Christ, and do what He says—John 14:15, 15:10)
- You shall love your neighbor as yourself. ("Golden rule" believers relationship to all men—Matthew 7:12, Luke 6:31).
- Love one another as I have loved you (this commandment only applies to the relationship between Christians-the Law of Christ).

> *1John 3:14-16:* [14] *We know that we have passed from death to life, because we love the brothers. He who does not love his brother abides in death.* [15] *Everyone hating his brother is a murderer. And you know that no murderer has everlasting life abiding in him.* [16] *By this we have known the love of God,*

because He laid down His life for us. And we ought to lay down our lives for the brothers. (MKJV)

To these 3 commandments, The Holy Spirit confirmed statutes for the Church to observe. They first appeared in the Council of Jerusalem where the Apostles and Elders ruled on what commandments the Gentile Christians should follow. In Matthew 5:17-18, the demand upon Jewish Christians required adherence to the Mosaic Law until it passed away. However, since the Mosaic Law did not pertain to Gentiles, what would Christ require of them in the New Covenant?

> *Act 15:24-31 (also Acts 21:25): (emphasis added)* [24] *Because we have heard that certain ones who went out from us have troubled you with words, unsettling your souls, saying, Be circumcised and keep the law!* **(to whom we gave no such command)**; [25] *it seemed good to us, being assembled with one accord, to send chosen men to you with our beloved Barnabas and Paul,* [26] *men who have given up their lives for the name of our Lord Jesus Christ.* [27] *Therefore we have sent Judas and Silas, who will also announce to you the same things by word.* [28] **For it seemed good to the Holy Spirit and to us to lay on you no greater burden than these necessary things:** [29] **that you abstain from meats offered to idols, and from blood, and from things strangled, and from fornication; from which, if you keep yourselves, you shall do well.** *Be prospered.* [30] *Then indeed they being let go, they came to Antioch. And gathering the multitude, they delivered the letter.* [31] **And when they had read it, they rejoiced at the comfort.** *(MKJV)*

The Council at Jerusalem passed down 3 statutes:
- Abstain from food offered to idols (worship)
- Don't eat strangled meat
- Abstain from sexual immorality

Scripture confirmed these 3 statutes thus fulfilling the law of the witness (Deuteronomy 19:15, John 8:17, Hebrews 10:28):

Revelation 2:12-14: (emphasis added) [12] *And to the angel of the church in Pergamos write: He who has the sharp sword with two edges says these things.* [13] *I know your works, and where you live, even where Satan's seat is. And you hold fast My name and have not denied My faith, even in those days in which Antipas was My faithful martyr, who was slain among you, where Satan dwells.* [14] ***But I have a few things against you, because you have there those who hold the teachings of Balaam, who taught Balak to cast a stumbling-block before the sons of Israel, to eat things sacrificed to idols and to commit fornication.*** *(MKJV)*

Revelation 2:18-22: (emphasis added) [18] *And to the angel of the church in Thyatira write: The Son of God, He who has His eyes like a flame of fire and His feet like burnished metal, says these things:* [19] *I know your works and love and service and faith and your patience, and your works; and the last to be more than the first.* [20] *But I have a few things against you because you allow that woman Jezebel to teach, she saying herself to be a prophetess, and* ***to cause My servants to go astray, and to commit fornication, and to eat idol-sacrifices.*** [21] *And I gave her time that she might repent of her fornication, and she did not repent.* [22] *Behold, I am throwing her into a bed, and those who commit adultery with her into great affliction, unless they repent of their deeds." (MKJV)*

Under the New Covenant, Christ replaces the burden of the Mosaic Law, the Prophets and Psalms with 3 commandments and 3 statutes. It is understandable why the Gentile Christians rejoiced at the ruling of the Apostles and brings meaning to the words of Jesus in Matthew 11:

Matthew 11:28-30: [28]*Come to Me, all you who labor and are heavy laden, and I will give you rest.* [29]*Take My yoke upon you and learn from Me, for I am gentle and lowly in heart, and you will find rest for your souls.* [30]*For my yoke is easy and My burden s light. (NKJV)*

CHAPTER 16   Divorce or Oneness

Let's revisit the issue of divorce. In chapter 14 I addressed the administration of the New Covenant must involve the actions of the Church individually as well as corporately. In chapter 8, in Jesus' discourse with the Pharisees, He reminded them of their hardness of heart regarding putting away a wife. The truth of the law of divorce in Mosaic Law finds fulfillment in God's redemption of Israel under a New Covenant. The Law of Moses made no provision for a man to remarry an unfaithful wife that he divorced and who remarried another husband. Through this law, God made clear that to remarry Israel the Old Covenant had to pass away so that a New Covenant might be established. Once again, the subject of Divorce and remarriage reveals God's intention to make for Himself a wife. Okay, so if divorce and remarriage reflects God's interaction with Israel, then how does the church rightly administer this subject to the world? Let's go to Matthew 19:

Matthew 19:3-6: ³ And the Pharisees came to Him, tempting Him and saying to Him, Is it lawful for a man to put away his wife for every cause? ⁴ And He answered and said to them, Have you not read that He who made them at the beginning "made them male and female," ⁵ and said, For this cause a man shall leave father and mother and shall cling to his wife, and the two of them shall be one flesh? ⁶ Therefore they are no longer two, but one flesh. Therefore what God has joined together, let not man separate. (MKJV)

To properly administer marriage, the goal of marriage must remain clear—marriage results in two becoming one. God is one. God and His church are one. Marriage is about a husband and wife becoming one. If the world fails to see a difference between itself and the Church, then the message of reconciliation goes unheeded. How many Christian marriages end in devastation, ruin, broken lives, and unrealized potential because they never learned to live as one together. Modern culture bombards our imaginations with romance and scripted love stories, based not in truth but the pursuit of emotional euphoria. Christians forget that God's love for His wife drove Him to endure great suffering to restore Her to Himself. We forget that marriage is about the journey to becoming one, the will to give and receive love when romance fades, and the joyful satisfaction that only comes from laying down your life for one another; just as Christ Jesus did for us:

> *Hebrews 12:1-3: (emphasis added) [1]Therefore since we also are surrounded with so great a cloud of witnesses, let us lay aside every weight and the sin which so easily besets us, and let us run with patience the race that is set before us, [2]looking to Jesus the Author and Finisher of our faith, **who for the joy that was set before Him endured the cross, despising the shame**, and sat down at the right of the throne of God. [3]For consider Him who endured such contradiction of sinners against Himself, **lest you be weary and faint in your minds**." (MKJV)*

In Matthew 19:6 Jesus gives this warning; *"Therefore what God has joined together, let not man separate." (MKJV)* Nowhere else in scripture will you find such emphatic innuendo of dire consequence. The covenantal joining of a man and woman for the purpose of oneness occupies such a place of holiness in God's mind that Christ warns all men, Christian as well as pagan—Don't you dare touch this. Marriage does not belong to the Church, we are its keepers and teachers. Marriage does not belong to the people to presumptuously redefine according to degenerate whims of fancy. Marriage most definitely does not belong to the state that perverts and manipulates issues of faith to accommodate political expediency. Marriage belongs to God and He holds it in the highest regard. The people, ministry, church, or denomination that presumes to redefine marriage does so at their own peril.

In Matthew 19:3-9 and Mark10:2-10 Jesus teaches the Jews about God's intentions to again be one with His people. How do we, as His wife, administer marriage to the world through our own marriages? I will attempt to answer this question in four parts:

- The Pharisees' question—Matthew. 19:3, Mark 10:2
- The command of the Mosaic Law—Matthew19:7-8, Mark 10:3-5
- The original intent of God—Matthew 19:4-6, Mark 10:6-9
- Jesus' command—Matthew 19:9, Mark 10:11-12

Firstly, when approaching this subject of divorce, the temptation to focus on the question of the Pharisees and the command of Jesus can take preeminence over the other parts. If we ignore the section in its entirety we risk missing the heart of God and perpetuating an injustice against certain members of the Church. I will be using the _King James Version_ exclusively in this section unless otherwise stated:

> _Matthew 19:3 (Mark 10:2) "The Pharisees also came unto him, tempting him, and saying unto him, Is it lawful for a man to put away his wife for every cause?"_

To truly understand Jesus' command we must first discern the question correctly. I know such a statement sounds overtly, if not insultingly obvious; yet, incorrect understanding and application of this text has nullified the potential of many in the Church. Many translations reflect a bias when translating the Greek word "apoluo" _(ap-ol-oo'-o)._ Both _Thayer's Greek Definitions_ and _Strong's Hebrew and Greek Dictionaries_ define this word as the King James and many reputable translations define it:

apoluō

1) to set free

2) to let go, dismiss, (to detain no longer)

    2a) a petitioner to whom liberty to depart is given by a decisive answer

    2b) **to bid depart, send away**

3) to let go free, release

    3a) a captive, i.e. to loose his bonds and bid him depart, to give him liberty to depart

    3b) to acquit one accused of a crime and set him at liberty

    3c) indulgently to grant a prisoner leave to depart

    3d) to release a debtor, i.e. not to press one's claim against him, to remit his debt

4) used of divorce, **to dismiss from the house, to repudiate**. The wife of a Greek or Roman may divorce her husband.

5) to send one's self away, to depart –*Thayer's Greek Definitions*

Thus to define this word as "put away," send away," or "dismiss" are all complimentary to the Greek. The following Translations define "apoluo" as "put away" or "dismiss" (I have included publishing dates to show agreement of translators over the centuries):

- American Standard Version (published 1901)
- Bishops Bible (published 1568)
- Geneva Bible (published 1560, 1587)
- Literal Translation of the Holy Bible (copyright 1976-2000, by Jay P Green)
- Modern King James Version (copyright 1962-1998, by Jay P Green)
- Young's literal Translation (published 1863, 1887, 1898)

In contrast, a large number of accepted translations agree with the *New King James Version* which translates "apoluo" as "divorce." Matthew 19:3— *"³The Pharisees also came to Him, testing Him, and saying to Him, 'is it lawful for a man to <u>divorce</u> his wife for just any reason?'"* (*NKJV*) The problem of translating the word "apoluo" as "divorce" will be explained in the second part.

> *Matt. 19:7-8 (Mark 10:3-5):* [7] *They say unto him, Why did Moses then command to give a writing of divorcement, and to put her away?* [8] *He saith unto them, Moses because of the hardness of your hearts suffered you to put away your wives: but from the beginning it was not so.*

Verse 7 uses the phrase "writing of divorcement." The Greek word used for divorcement is the word "apostasion" (*ap-os-tas'-ee-on*). Again, both *Thayer's Greek Definitions*, and *Strong's Hebrew and Greek Dictionaries* agree on its meaning:

apostasion
1) divorce, repudiation
2) a bill of divorce—*Thayer's Greek Definitions*

Secondly, according to Mosaic Law (Deuteronomy 24:1-4), a man was not permitted to simply dismiss or put away his wife. The Law demanded a man first place in her hand a legal document referred to as a "writing of divorcement" and then send her away. The word "divorce" or "divorcement" never appears alone in the *King James Version*, it is always preceded by the term "writing" or "bill." In Matthew 19:3-9 the term "writing (bill) of divorcement" only appears in the Greek in verse 7 in reference to the Law of Moses. In Mark 10:2-12 the term "bill (writing) of divorcement" only appears in the Greek once in verse 4 in reference to the Law of Moses. All other Greek words pertaining to the subject in this discourse are correctly translated "put away" or "dismiss." The attempt by the Pharisees to tempt Jesus rests in the proper translation of the question, "*The Pharisees also came unto him, tempting him, and saying unto him, **Is it lawful for a man to put away his wife for every cause?***" Jesus, aware of their attempt, forces them to recall the Law of Moses. Through the Mosaic Law, Jesus forces the Pharisees to confess their error regarding the

question. No, it is not lawful to put away your wife without a
bill of divorcement!

In verse 8 Jesus confronts the hardness of heart of the men of
Israel. Although the "hardness of your hearts" term Jesus used
could refer to Israel's hardness toward God, I believe the
reference pointed to the men's view of their wives. Because the
men of Israel did not receive their wives as one with them, they
saw their wives as means to an end. Maybe the men gained
wealth or status through marriage. Maybe they reduced
marriage to only a legal means to have sex, or a means of
raising sons. Whatever the reason, when their wife no longer
pleased them, the husbands used "putting away" as a weapon
against their wives. This tool of manipulation and intimidation
meant that a woman "put away" without a "bill of
divorcement" still remained married under the Law. She could
not remarry under penalty of death, however being cast out of
her home without any means of support meant destitution.
Needless to say, especially for God-fearing women, trying to
support oneself alone in a male-dominated society made such
abominable professions as prostitution very tempting. God
actually confronts the men of Israel over this perversion of His
Law in Malachi 2:

> *Malachi 2:13-16: (emphasis added)* ^{13} *And this is a second
> thing you have done, covering the altar of Jehovah with tears,
> weeping, and groaning, yet not facing toward the food
> offering, and taking it with delight from your hand.* ^{14} *Yet you
> say, Why?* **Because Jehovah has been witness between you
> and the wife of your youth, against whom you have dealt
> treacherously**; *yet she is your companion and your covenant
> wife.* ^{15} *And did He not make you one? Yet the vestige of the
> Spirit is in him. And what of the one? He was seeking a godly
> seed.* **Then guard your spirit, and do not act
> treacherously with the wife of your youth.** ^{16} *Jehovah, the
> God of Israel, says* **He hates sending away**; *and to cover with*

violence on his garment, says Jehovah of Hosts. Then guard
your spirit, and do not act treacherously. (MKJV)

Thirdly, Malachi revealed the purpose behind the Law of
Moses, that is, the Law of Moses addressed conduct while
revealing the corruption in the heart of man. This corruption of
heart could not be changed through Mosaic Law, that work was
reserved for the Messiah who initiated a New Covenant. So
when Jesus responds to the Pharisees question, He adds the
truth of marriage I will address in part three.

> *Matthew 19:4-6 (Mark 10:6-9): ⁴ And he answered and said*
> *unto them, Have ye not read, that he which made them at the*
> *beginning made them male and female, ⁵ And said, For this*
> *cause shall a man leave father and mother, and shall cleave*
> *to his wife: and they twain shall be one flesh? ⁶ Wherefore*
> *they are no more twain, but one flesh. What therefore God*
> *hath joined together, let not man put asunder.*

As stated before, two becoming one is the foundation of
marriage. Oneness between a husband and his wife reflects the
intention of God to be one with man. God also points to this
fact in the previous quote from Malachi 2:15 *"And did He not*
make you one? Yet the vestige of the Spirit is in him. And what of
the one? He was seeking a godly seed. Then guard your spirit,
and do not act treacherously with the wife of your youth."
(MKJV) Therefore, if God's purpose for marriage was oneness,
then what should be the purpose for marriage in the Church.
Maybe, if we taught our children and new believers the
foundational truth of marriage, then divorce statistics in the
Church would drop to insignificance. If our words of being one
in Christ reflected in our oneness with our spouse, then
wouldn't the world find attraction to our witness. Thus the
Church fulfills Her role to rightly administer marriage. Now,
having covered these three points regarding divorce, I believe
the fourth point can clearly be understood.

Matthew 19:9 " And I say unto you, Whosoever shall put away his wife, except it be for fornication, and shall marry another, committeth adultery: and whoso marrieth her which is put away doth commit adultery."

Here is the answer to the Pharisees question, *"Is it lawful for a man to put away his wife for every cause?"* However, the context of the discourse gives so much more meaning:

- The Law gives no allowance for a man to put away his wife.
- The Law only allows for divorce if "uncleanness" is found—Deut. 24:1-4
- The Law demands a legal "bill of divorcement" before putting away a wife, thus freeing her from accusation of adultery, and allows her to be married to another.
- Malachi 2:13-16 teaches that the marriage covenant demands a husband be one with his wife and not use the threat of divorce to mistreat her.
- Malachi 2:13-16 judges that a man refusing to be one with his wife and instead deals treacherously with her, actually betrays the Spirit of God in him.
- Jesus reminds us that marriage is about oneness, therefore, refusing to be one is to be in violation of the Spirit of God in us.
- If a husband and wife refuse to become one through the hardness of heart toward one another, then they should be free through divorce rather than be tempted to commit adultery.
- To marry another (or to become one with another) that is "put away" and not divorced is to commit adultery.
- To commit fornication is to break the covenant of marriage.
- To actually go through the legal process of divorce is to be compliant with the Law given by God.

To make these statements is not to justify or endorse divorce as the solution to problems in marriage. Just as marriage exists as an incredible, life-altering choice, divorce exists as a tragic and life-altering choice. It tears apart families and creates long-term problems in children. It tarnishes reputations, destroys dreams, and halts potential. Divorce is the tearing apart of one to make two, and just like the splitting of the atom, totally destructive—just as God designed it. How naive to think that divorce can happen without dire consequences. God's divorce of Israel resulted in the fall of a nation, countless deaths, the wiping out of entire families, and myriads of people put into slavery. We should not be so arrogant as to believe that we can transgress the Spirit of God in us and escape judgment. If God suffered through His divorce, so would anyone else.

As the Church, we must remind each other who we are, who we represent, and the responsibility we have to God to administer His Marriage Covenant to the world. If we do not rightly fulfill our role to teach and administer marriage before the world, then we must repent. Marriage is oneness; we reflect our oneness with our God through our oneness in marriage. If we do not reflect oneness in marriage then we contradict the Spirit of God in us.

CHAPTER 17   The Law of Christ

As stated before, there exists both an individual and a corporate element to the Church's role as wife under the New Covenant. Although this book looks at different facets of this New Marriage Covenant, the Covenant itself rest on one single word—love.

- God is love
- God's love for man
- God's love for Israel
- Israel's love for her neighbors
- God's love for His wife
- Christ's love for His Church
- The Church's love for Her neighbors (those outside the New Covenant)
- The Church's love for one another (those inside the New Covenant)

Let's look at the last point; the Church's love one for another. As you can see, the relationship between God and Israel reflects the relationship between Christ and His church similarly; except at this point of love between members. The similarities come from the two great commandments:

- Love God with all your heart, soul, mind, and strength.
- Love your neighbor as yourself.

These two commandments form the foundation of Christian ministry to our world. As Christians, we choose to demonstrate our love for God through acts of charity, proclaiming the gospel of Christ, even suffering personally to love our neighbors into the Kingdom of God. From these pursuits the Church founded powerful ministries like the Salvation Army, Voice of the Martyrs, Union Gospel Missions, Samaritan's Purse, and other denominational and inter-denominational organizations.

These pursuits are good and right, demonstrating God's love to the world and showing the glory God gave to the Church. However, there exists only one law, one commandment, given by the Lord Jesus Christ that identifies those that are His. Throughout His ministry, Jesus taught and reaffirmed the two great commandments (Matthew 22:37-40, Mark 12:28-31); yet on the night He initiated the New Covenant, Jesus gave the third commandment.

> *John 13:33-35:* ^{*33*} *Little children, I am with you yet a little while. You shall seek Me; and as I said to the Jews, Where I go, you cannot come, so I now say to you.* ^{*34*} *I give you a new commandment, that you love one another. As I have loved you, you should also love one another.* ^{*35*} *By this all shall know that you are My disciples, if you have love toward one another. (MKJV)*

And again in John 15:

> *John 15:10-12:* ^{*10*} *If you keep My commandments, you shall abide in My love, even as I have kept My Father's commandments and abide in His love.* ^{*11*} *I have spoken these things to you so that My joy might remain in you and your joy might be full.*^{*12*} *This is My commandment, that you love one another as I have loved you. (MKJV)*

In John's epistles to the Church he brings to remembrance the command of Christ:

> *1John 2:8-11:* ^{*8*} *Again, I write a new commandment to you, which thing is true in Him and in you, because the darkness is passing away, and the true Light now shines.* ^{*9*} *He who says he is in the light and hates his brother is in darkness until now.* ^{*10*}*He who loves his brother abides in the light, and there is no offense in him.* ^{*11*} *But he who hates his brother is in darkness, and walks in darkness, and does not know where he is going, because darkness has blinded his eyes. (MKJV)*

1 John 3:10-24: (emphasis added) ¹⁰ *In this the children of God are revealed, and the children of the Devil:* **everyone not practicing righteousness is not of God, also he who does not love his brother.** ¹¹ *For this is the message that you have heard from the beginning,* **that we should love one another;** ¹² *not as Cain who was of the evil one, and killed his brother. And for what did he kill him? Because his own works were evil, and his brother's things were righteous.* ¹³ *Do not marvel, my brothers, if the world hates you.* ¹⁴ **We know that we have passed from death to life, because we love the brothers.** *He who does not love his brother abides in death.* ¹⁵**Everyone hating his brother is a murderer.** *And you know that no murderer has everlasting life abiding in him.* ¹⁶*By this we have known the love of God, because He laid down His life for us. And we ought to lay down our lives for the brothers* ¹⁷*But whoever has this world's goods and sees his brother having need, and shuts up his bowels from him, how does the love of God dwell in him?* ¹⁸*My children, let us not love in word or in tongue, but in deed and in truth.* ¹⁹*And in this we shall know that we are of the truth, and shall assure our hearts before Him,* ²⁰ *that if our heart accuses us, God is greater than our heart and knows all things.* ²¹*Beloved, if our heart does not accuse us, we have confidence toward God.* ²² *And whatever we ask, we receive from Him, because we keep His commandments and do those things that are pleasing in His sight.* ²³**And this is His commandment, that we should believe on the name of His Son Jesus Christ, and love one another, as He gave us commandment.** ²⁴*And he who keeps His commandment dwells in Him, and He in him. And by this we know that He abides in us, by the Spirit which He gave to us. (MKJV)*

1 John 4:20-21: ²⁰ *If anyone says, I love God, and hates his brother, he is a liar. For if he does not love his brother whom he has seen, how can he love God whom he has not seen?*

²¹And we have this commandment from Him, that he who loves God should love his brother also." (MKJV)

Surely, these passages are familiar to all Christians and my purpose in extensively quoting them was not to fill the page. The epistles of the Apostle John draw more attention to Christ's law than to the other commandments. So how does this new commandment given by Christ differ from the other two? How do we apply and obey it?

First of all, remember that this commandment directly ties to the New Covenant. Therefore the commandment of Christ determines who takes part in the New Marriage Covenant and who does not. Those that obey the commandments of Christ are part of the wife that God formed from His own flesh. To not walk in the same love for the body that Christ did denies the profession of our faith; as John says, "If anyone says, I love God, and hates his brother, he is a liar." So it's important to understand and practice this commandment of Christ.

In the writings of Paul, he deals with real life examples of both the second commandment (love your neighbor as yourself) and commandment of Christ (love one another as I have loved you).

Galatians 5:13-15: ¹³For, brothers, you were called to liberty. Only do not use the liberty for an opening to the flesh, but by love serve one another. ¹⁴ For all the Law is fulfilled in one word, even in this, "You shall love your neighbor as yourself." ¹⁵ But if you bite and devour one another, take heed that you are not consumed by one another." (MKJV)

Paul reminds the Galatians that by treating others like they want to be treated not only keeps the Old Covenant Mosaic Law, but actually fulfills it; just as Jesus said He came to do in Matthew 5:17.

Galatians 6:2-- Bear one another's burdens, and so you will fulfill the Law of Christ. (MKJV)

This challenge by Paul promotes a lifestyle unique to Christianity because it is unique to Christ. Where the second commandment focuses on mutual respect and peaceful interaction between men, the Law of Christ emphasizes personal sacrifice for those within the church established by Christ. The Law of Christ demands that those called by His name prove their love for Him by sacrificing themselves for others called by His name. Remember that we were undeserving of Christ's love, even considered His enemy (Colossians 1:19-21); therefore following the Law of Christ demonstrates its greatest power when the potential of strife exists between members. Consider the following:

John 13:13-17: ¹³You call Me the Teacher, and Lord, and you say well, for I AM. ¹⁴If then I, the Lord and the Teacher, have washed your feet, you also ought to wash one another's feet. ¹⁵ For I have given you an example, that you should do as I have done to you. ¹⁶Truly, truly, I say to you, A servant is not greater than his master, neither is he who is sent greater than he who sent him. ¹⁷If you know these things, blessed are you if you do them. (MKJV)

Romans 15:1-3: ¹Then we who are strong ought to bear the infirmities of the weak, and not to please ourselves. ²Let every one of us please his neighbor for his good, to building up. ³For even Christ did not please Himself; but as it is written, "The reproaches of those who reproached You fell on Me. (MKJV)

1 Corinthians 8:9-12: ⁹But take heed lest by any means this liberty of yours becomes a stumbling block to those who are weak. ¹⁰For if anyone sees you who have knowledge sitting in an idol temple, will not the weak one's conscience be lifted up so as to eat things sacrificed to idols? ¹¹And on your knowledge the weak brother will fall, he for whom Christ died. [12]And sinning in this way against your brothers, and wounding their conscience, being weak, you sin against Christ. (MKJV)

Galatians 6:1-3: [1]Brothers, if a man is overtaken in a fault, you the spiritual ones restore such a one in the spirit of meekness, considering yourself, lest you also be tempted. [2]Bear one another's burdens, and so you will fulfill the Law of Christ. [3]For if anyone thinks himself to be something, being nothing, he deceives himself." (MKJV)

1 Corinthians 6:1-8: (emphasis added) **[1]Do any of you dare, when you have a matter against another, to go to law before the unjust, and not before the saints?** *[2]Do you not know that the saints shall judge the world? And if the world shall be judged by you, are you unworthy to judge the smallest matters? [3]Do you not know that we shall judge angels, not to mention the things of this life? [4]If, then, you truly have judgments of the things of this life, set those who are least esteemed in the church to judge. [5]For I speak to your shame. Is it so that there is not a wise one among you, not even one in your midst who shall be able to judge between his brother?* **[6]But brother goes to law with brother, and that before the unbelievers. [7]Indeed then there is already on the whole a failure among you, that you have lawsuits with yourselves. Why not instead be wronged? Why not instead be defrauded? [8]But you do wrong and defraud, and these things to brothers.** *(MKJV)*

So how does this understanding of the Law of Christ apply to the issues of marriage today? I say that it must be applied between husband and wife, between individual members of the church, and between church congregations themselves.

Marriage between Christian husbands and wives demands moral purity, yet the Law of Christ also makes demands in the relationship itself. Remember, as Christians we carry the revelation of marriage to the rest of the world as Jesus proclaimed in John 13:35, "By this all shall know that you are My disciples, if you have love toward one another." The obedience to the Law of Christ proclaims the love of Christ to those who do not yet believe. They are watching us, do they have a clear example of who Christ is? Go back to Ephesians. 5:22-33 and read it again in the new understanding you have regarding marriage. The interaction between husband and wife stated in Ephesians 5, according to Paul, is actually the interaction between Christ and His Church. However, the example of Christ and His Church given in Ephesians 5, also according to Paul, reflects how Christian husbands and wives should demonstrate their love. Look at the reality of Christ and His church; then apply that truth to our marriages and let Christ bring a whole new meaning to our marriage roles. Why does the Church submit to Christ, because she loves Him. Yet it was Christ that loved first, and the Church responded in kind.

As husbands before Christ, men do not demand love from their wives, they initiate love. Christ never demanded love, he demonstrated it by laying down His life. Those that responded to His love he received into His New Covenant and made them one with His body; teaching them to love as He loved. As wives before Christ, women submit to their husbands in response to the love shown them. With this display of love and submission in marriage, Christ reinforces with His Law, "love one another as I have loved you." Husbands and wives laying down their lives for one another; forgiving, forbearing, sacrificing, enduring, committing and submitting to each other. Can there be any greater demonstration of God's love and intention to all men than when Christians demonstrate the Law of Christ.

This same Law of Christ demonstrated in marriage also applies
to the Church individually and corporately:

- Individual believers lay down their lives for one
  another, preferring one another and bearing one
  another up, even to the point of personal cost or
  injury-- Just as Christ did for us.

- The believers strong in faith and wisdom showing
  gentleness and compassion to the weaker and less
  wise—Just as Christ did for us.

- The less desirable or weaker members of the body
  being surrounded and protected by the stronger
  members; even to the point of personal cost or
  injury—Just as Christ did for us.

- Congregations looking to do good to congregations
  outside their accepted and practiced distinctives and
  doctrines.—Just as Christ did for us.

- Congregations accepting the generosity and good will
  of other congregations outside their accepted
  distinctives and doctrines.

- Congregations supporting other congregations in
  trouble; even to the point of personal cost or injury to
  reputation.—Just as Christ did for us.

- Congregations in a region proclaiming themselves as
  one, defined by the Law of Christ and not their
  accepted distinctives and doctrines.

If the fulfillment of marriage, as Jesus and Paul defines it, is
oneness; and the purpose of the New Covenant is oneness;
then how can any believer or group of believers condone
division. What kind of demonstration does today's world see in
Christianity. The airwaves and internet overflow with "come to
Jesus" messages proclaiming the love of God and songs of
"come as you are" declaring His grace and mercy. Yet when one
believes and crosses the threshold into the local church, they
are not taught about "love God, love your neighbor, love the

brethren as Christ loved you." New believers are swept into a maelstrom of doctrinal and cultural distinctives that confuse the culture of that particular church or denomination with the Law of Christ. Add to that the carnal desire of religious partisanship and the simplicity and beauty that is the New Marriage Covenant gets twisted and perverted into a false representation of Christ to the new believer. Dare we consider the words of Christ Himself when confronting the perversions of the Pharisees:

> Matthew 23:15-- *Woe to you, scribes and Pharisees, hypocrites! For you compass sea and the dry land to make one proselyte, and when he is made, you make him twofold more the child of hell than yourselves. (MKJV)*

Is it any wonder that the Church is openly mocked, not for its doctrine or message (as in the early church), but for the rampant hypocrisy and misrepresentation of the Gospel that Christ preached. Is it any wonder that more believers lose faith because the Law of Christ gets buried under the heaps of discarded lives left behind by charismatic self-serving ministries? Is it any wonder that more believers don't share their faith because they must spend more effort and energy trying to defend the church than introduce the New Covenant? Is it any wonder when Christian marriages fail because husbands and wives obsess over their needs rather than follow the example set by Christ? Where is the love? Where is the unity? What has happened to the oneness delivered to us by the ministry, suffering and resurrection of Christ Jesus? Does the world recognize us as those who are one with Christ Jesus, or just the heralds of another "path to God"?

It is long past time to remind ourselves of what it means to be one in Christ. It is time to reintroduce the Law of Christ to the church; both in instruction, and most importantly in demonstration.

CHAPTER 18   Throw Down Jezebel

I started this final section by recalling Jesus' example of love demonstrated through obedience. Obedience to God's commandments is the only true demonstration of love for God. Obedience to God revealed the Messiah and only obedience to Messiah reveals the true Church, "If you love Me, keep My commandments." Many voices inside the Church attempt to influence Church culture by using terms like "inclusiveness", "tolerance", "acceptance", or "seeker-friendly". By grouping these loaded words with love towards God, these groups and individuals try to redefine what God's love means. Once successful in redefining God's love, pressure comes to bear on the Christian community to retreat from condemning sexual immorality in all its forms. These false ministers even endorse the very deviancy held in reproach by Scripture. Sadly, many in the Church have been deceived by this perversion of what it means to love God and walk in His love. God does not define His love by the emotional whimsy of man's self-righteousness. God is love, Christ is one with the Father and the Church is one with Christ. Therefore, the Church is one with God's love and charged by Her husband to be the mystery revealed to the rest of the world through faithfulness and obedience to His commandments. So defining the love of God to the world rests not in emotional ambiguity but as a decision marked by action. Let's look at how God responds to His Church when She wanes in Her love for Her husband.

In the second and third chapters of Revelation, the revealed Christ addresses 7 churches in Asia. 2 of these churches receive approval and encouragement from the Lord; however, 5 of the churches receive rebuke and warning. Christ addresses the seven churches directly with instruction to the Church as a whole:

Revelation 2:23--...and all the churches will know that I am He who searches the reins and hearts, and I will give to every one of you according to your works. (NKJV)

The Lord Jesus Christ meant that the words spoken to the churches in Revelation be taken to heart by all the Church. In all seven churches the Lord directly addressed issues regarding the marriage covenant between Himself and the Church:

- Ephesus (Rev. 2:1-7)—In spite of Her good works the Lord accused Her of leaving Her first love, Her husband. He threatened to come quickly and remove Her light if she did not repent.

- Smyrna (Rev. 2:8-11)—A faithful church with good works that endured, and would endure tribulation. The Lord encouraged them in their marriage faithfulness, "Be faithful until death, and I will give you the crown of life."; and "He who overcomes shall not be hurt by the second death."

- Pergamos (Rev. 2:12-17)—Although Pergamos demonstrated faithfulness to her husband, they allowed the teaching of sexual immorality in the Church. The false teaching stood as a direct assault on the statutes given the Gentile churches in Acts 15:19-20 and 21:25. The Lord warned Pergamos to repent and cast out the false teachers or else share in their imminent judgment.

- Sardis (Rev. 3:1-6)—Sardis resembled Old Covenant Israel. They claimed to be alive but were dead and dying, being spared only by the few undefiled ones among them. The Lord warns Sardis of His imminent coming, to repent and follow the example of the undefiled ones. Only the undefiled ones received the promise of white garments and Christ proclaiming their names from the Book of Life before the Father and the angels.

- Philadelphia (Rev. 3:7-13)—This Church along with Smyrna, received a glowing commendation from Her Lord. Philadelphia receives praise for Her faithfulness and obedience. The Lord professes His love and intentions toward Her with great anticipation and imminence.

- Laodicea (Rev. 3:14-22)—Laodicea also followed the example of Old Covenant Israel. She considered Herself rich and in need of nothing; indifferent and lukewarm toward Her husband. Just as Israel was left naked, wounded, and destitute, the Lord extends the same warning to Laodicea. The Lord declared Laodicea wretched, naked and poor yet His love for Her compelled Him to rebuke Her that she might repent. He then proposes to Her again as He did in the Song of Solomon:

Song of Solomon 5:2-4: ²I sleep, but my heart is awake. It is the sound of my Beloved that knocks, saying, Open to Me, My sister, My love, My dove, My undefiled; for My head is filled with dew, My locks with the drops of the night. ³I have put off My coat; How shall I put it on? I have washed my feet; how shall I defile them? ⁴My Beloved put in His hand by the hole of the door, and my heart was moved for Him." (MKJV)

The relationship between God and Old Covenant Israel reflects the relationship between Christ and His Church in Revelation. The Church of Thyatira offers a beneficial look into the subject of faithfulness to Christ and His intention to be an active participant in preserving Her virtue.

*Rev 2:18-23: (emphasis added) ¹⁸And to the angel of the church in Thyatira write: The Son of God, He who has His eyes like a flame of fire and His feet like burnished metal, says these things: ¹⁹I know your works and love and service and faith and your patience, and your works; and the last to be more than the first. ²⁰**But I have a few things against you because you allow that woman Jezebel to teach, she saying herself to be a prophetess, and to cause My servants to go astray, and to commit fornication, and to eat idol-sacrifices. ²¹And I gave her time that she might repent of her fornication, and she did not repent. ²²Behold, I am throwing her into a bed, and those who commit adultery with her into great affliction, unless*** *they repent of their deeds.* ²³*And I will kill her children with death. And all the churches will know that I am He who searches the reins and hearts, and I will give to every one of you according to your works." (MKJV)*

The Lord starts by praising Her good works but moves on to confront Her adultery. The reference in verse 20 to Jezebel should immediately remind the reader of the wicked Queen of Israel in First and Second Kings: (emphasis added)

> *1Kings 16:30-31:* ³⁰*And Ahab the son of Omri did evil in the sight of Jehovah above all who were before him.* ³¹*And as if it had been a light thing for him to walk in the sins of Jeroboam the son of Nebat,* **he also took Jezebel, the daughter of Ethbaal king of the Sidonians, for a wife. And he went and served Baal, and worshiped him.** *(MKJV)*

> *1Kings 18:3-4:* ³*And Ahab called Obadiah, who was over the house. (And Obadiah feared Jehovah greatly,* ⁴*for it happened when* **Jezebel cut off the prophets of Jehovah,** *Obadiah took a hundred prophets and hid them by fifty in a cave, and fed them with bread and water.) (MKJV)*

> *1Ki 21:23-25:* ²³*And Jehovah also spoke of Jezebel saying, "The dogs shall eat Jezebel by the wall of Jezreel.* ²⁴*He who dies of Ahab in the city, the dogs shall eat. And he who dies in the field, the birds of the air shall eat".* ²⁵**But there was none like Ahab, who sold himself to work wickedness in the sight of Jehovah, whom Jezebel his wife stirred up.** *(MKJV)*

> *2Ki 9:22-24:* ²²*And it happened when Jehoram saw Jehu, he said, "Is it peace, Jehu?" And he answered,* **"What peace, so long as the harlotries of your mother Jezebel and her witchcrafts are so many?"** ²³*And Jehoram turned his hands and fled and said to Ahaziah, "Treachery, Ahaziah!"* ²⁴**And Jehu drew a bow and struck Jehoram between his arms,**

and the arrow went out at his heart, and he sank down in his chariot. (MKJV)

2Ki 9:30-37: *[30]And Jehu had come to Jezreel. And Jezebel heard, and had painted her face and adorned her head, and looked out at a window. [31]And Jehu came to the gate. And she said,"Was it peace to Zimri the slayer of his lord?" [32]And he lifted up his face to the window, and said, "Who is with me? Who?" And two or three eunuchs looked out at him. [33]**And he said, "Throw her down!" And they threw her down.** And some of her blood was sprinkled on the wall and on the horses. And he trampled her. [34]And when he had come in, he ate and drank, and said, "Go, now see this cursed woman and bury her. For she is a king's daughter." [35]**And they went to bury her, but they found no more of her than the skull and the feet and the palms of** her **hands.** [36]And they came again and told him. And he said, "This is the Word of Jehovah which He spoke by His servant Elijah the Tishbite, saying, In the portion of Jezreel the dogs shall eat the flesh of Jezebel. [37]**And the dead body of Jezebel shall be as dung on the face of the field in the portion of Jezreel, so that they shall not say, This is Jezebel.**" (MKJV)*

Whether the reference to Jezebel in Revelation refers to an actual woman in the Thyatiran Church, or an attitude, or a doctrine is speculative. The important point of the warning lies in the connection between God's contempt towards the historical Jezebel and the Jezebel of Revelation. This connection must be taken seriously by all in the Church, to preserve the members from suffering the same judgment.

Historical Jezebel—

- An ungodly woman gaining influence through manipulation and deceit: *"... he also took Jezebel, the daughter of Eth-baal king of the Sidonians, for a wife. And he went and served Baal, and worshiped him."*

- Tried to systematically destroy the prophets of God: *"...for it happened when Jezebel cut off the prophets of Jehovah..."*

- Used her power and influence to turn Israel to idolatry and commit fornication against God: *"But there was none like Ahab, who sold himself to work wickedness in the sight of Jehovah, whom Jezebel his wife stirred up."*

- God overthrows her and destroys her: *"And he said, Throw her down! And they threw her down."; "And they went to bury her, but they found no more of her than the skull and the feet and the palms of her hands."*

- God kills her son because of her wickedness: *"...What peace, so long as the harlotries of your mother Jezebel and her witchcrafts are so many?"; "And Jehu drew a bow and struck Jehoram between his arms, and the arrow went out at his heart, and he sank down in his chariot."*

Revelation's Jezebel—

- A presumptive woman that gained influence through manipulation and deceit: *"But I have a few things against you because you allow that woman Jezebel to teach, she saying herself to be a prophetess..."*

- Brought dishonor upon the prophetic office by convincing those in Thyatira she was a prophet: *"...you allow that woman Jezebel to teach, she saying herself to be a prophetess..."*

- Used her power and influence to turn the Church of Thyatira to idolatry and commit fornication: *"But I have a few things against you because you allow that woman Jezebel to teach, she saying herself to be a prophetess, and to cause My servants to go astray, and to commit fornication, and to eat idol-sacrifices."*

- God promises to overthrow and destroy her: *"And I gave her time that she might repent of her fornication, and she did not repent. Behold, I am throwing her into a bed, and those who commit adultery with her into great affliction, unless they repent of their deeds."*

- God promises to kill her children: *"And I will kill her children with death."*

The Jezebel reference in Revelation 2:18-23 sheds light on God's definition of sexual immorality. Idolatry and sexual immorality are the same thing to God, disobedience to God's Law and idolatry are the same thing. Therefore, to disobey the Law of God is to commit idolatry against Him; which God equates to committing fornication against Him. The letter to Thyatira also reveals how God holds those in authority over the church, whether legitimate or not, to greater accountability and judgment.

The letter to Thyatira ends with this warning, "And all the churches will know that I am He who searches the reins and hearts, and I will give to every one of you according to your works." It's way past time to stop being so tolerant of sexual immorality in the Church. It's time to stop interpreting the Law of God as cultural and therefore irrelevant for today. It's time to stop abdicating our God-given authority as the Church to legislatures. It's time to stop allowing false-teachers and self-proclaimed prophets redefine faithfulness to God. It's time to stop treating the love and grace of our Lord with indifference. It's time the Church took to heart the warnings of God and realize that God's Wife serves in faithfulness and Godliness. Those that betray Him and lead others into unfaithfulness have no place in His kingdom. We must repent, individually and corporately, from our indifference to His Covenant. Return to our First Love, and experience His favor rather than His anger. Remember His mercy lasts forever, unless we become His enemy.

CHAPTER 19   The Faithful Wife

Ephesians 5:31-33: [31]For this cause a man shall leave his father and mother and shall be joined to his wife, and the two of them shall be one flesh." [32]This is a great mystery, but I speak concerning Christ and the church. [33]But also let everyone of you in particular so love his wife even as himself, and the wife that she defers to her husband." (MKJV)

As His Church, Christians carry the answer to the ancient mystery—what does marriage mean? To married Christians, we share the added privilege of living our married lives in love to Christ and to each other. Our oneness in marriage demonstrates our oneness with Christ to the world. Only through oneness with Christ can there be oneness with God, only through oneness with God do we have eternal life.

Outside of marriage, the love displayed among Christians also answers the great mystery. When we lay down our lives for one another and forbear with each other we show our oneness with Christ, fulfilling His commandment. Therefore, consider the admonition of Paul in Ephesians:

Ephesians 4:1-6: [1]I therefore, the prisoner in the Lord, beseech you that you walk worthy of the calling with which you are called, [2]with all lowliness and meekness, with long-suffering, forbearing one another in love, [3]endeavoring to keep the unity of the Spirit in the bond of peace. [4]There is one body and one Spirit, even as you are called in one hope of your calling, [5]one Lord, one faith, one baptism, [6]one God and Father of all, who is above all and through all and in you all." (MKJV)

And again in 2 Thessalonians,

2 Thessalonians 1:11-12: [11]Therefore we also pray always for you that our God would count you worthy of the calling and fulfill all the good pleasure of His goodness and the work of faith with power, [12]that the name of our Lord Jesus Christ may be glorified in you, and you in Him, according to the grace of our God and the Lord Jesus Christ." (MKJV)

How great is the love of God towards those who believe; and how simple to understand His expectations of us:

3 Laws of New Covenant, the Law of the Spirit
1. Love the Lord with all your heart, soul, mind and strength. (Mat. 22:37)
2. Love your neighbor as yourself. (Mat. 22:39, Mat. 7:12, Rom. 13:8-10)
3. Love the brethren as Christ loved you. (John 13:34, 1Ti. 1:5-8)

3 ordinances of abstinence, commands given by the apostles (Acts 15:28-29, Acts 21:25, Rev. 2:18-20)
1. Abstain from food offered to idols
2. Abstain from strangled meats
3. Abstain from sexual immorality.

The simplicity of the New Covenant, this Marriage Covenant, displays the love and genius of God. By living these 3 laws and 3 ordinances, as demonstrated by Christ and the Apostles, we participate in the revealing of the great mystery to all creation.

In the letters to the 7 churches of Revelation, the Lord ended each letter with a promise of blessing to those that remained faithful to Him. The key word is "overcome" which John himself defines in his epistle:

1 John 5:3-5: (emphasis added) [3]For this is the love of God, that we keep His commandments, and His commandments are not burdensome. [4]For everything that has been born of

God overcomes the world. **And this is the victory that**
overcomes the world, our faith. *⁵Who is he who*
overcomes the world, but he who believes that Jesus is
the Son of God?" *(MKJV)*

So as you read these promises from Revelation know that to
love God, obey His commandments, keep the faith, and believe
that Jesus is the Son of God, defines overcoming the world:
(emphasis added)

- Ephesus--Rev 2:7-- *"He who has an ear, let him hear*
  what the Spirit says to the churches. To him who
  overcomes **I will give to eat of the Tree of Life, which**
  is in the midst of the paradise of God." *(MKJV)*
- Smyrna--Rev 2:11-- *"He who has an ear, let him hear*
  what the Spirit says to the churches. He who overcomes
  will not be hurt by the second death." *(MKJV)*
- Pergamus--Rev 2:17-- *"He who has an ear, let him hear*
  what the Spirit says to the churches. To him who
  overcomes **I will give to eat of the hidden manna, and**
  will give to him a white stone, and in the stone a new
  name written, which no man knows except he who
  receives it." *(MKJV)*
- Thyatira—Rev. 2:26-29: *²⁶ And he who overcomes and*
  keeps My works to the end, to **him I will give power**
  over the nations. *²⁷* **And he will rule them with a rod**
  of iron, as the vessels of a potter the will be broken to
  pieces, even as I received from My Father. *²⁸* **And I**
  will give him the Morning Star.²⁹ *He who has an ear,*
  let him hear what the spirit says to the churches. *(MKJV)*
- Sardis--Rev 3:5-6 : *⁵ The one who overcomes,* **this one**
  will be clothed in white clothing. And I will not blot
  out his name out of the Book of Life, but I will confess
  his name before My Father and before His angels. *⁶*
  He who has an ear, let him hear what the Spirit says to
  the churches." *(MKJV)*

- Philadelphia--Rev 3:12-13 *"Him who overcomes **I will make him a pillar in the temple of My God, and he will go out no more. And I will write upon him the name of My God, and the name of the city of My God, the New Jerusalem, which comes down out of Heaven from My God, and My new name.** :[13] He who has an ear, let him hear what the Spirit says to the churches."* (MKJV)

- Laodicea--Rev 3:21-22: [21] *To him who overcomes **I will grant to sit with Me in My throne, even as I also overcame and have sat down with My Father in His throne.*** [22] *He who has an ear, let him hear what the Spirit says to the churches."* (MKJV)

The love of God is the origin of His faithfulness toward us who believe. In response, our faithfulness to Him demonstrates our love and secures our participation in these promises.

Therefore, in light of these great promises, let us remind ourselves of this great love of God. Remember again the great suffering endured by almighty God from before time began, to create for Himself a people for His name. Remember that God fully committed Himself to the process of making for Himself a wife, a helpmate suitable to Himself. Be reminded that He became flesh and bone, submitting Himself to the wrath of inferiors that He might make a New Creation, a wife from His own body, a great mystery revealed through His Christ. Be reminded again that God did all this that He might have a family, a wife and children to share the wonders of His kingdom as an inheritance.

Let us, the body of Christ, regard again this sacred Covenant with the reverence it deserves. It is right that we humble ourselves before our Lord and confess our ignorance, arrogance and indifference. If we confess to Him our sins, He will forgive us. Repent from doing evil and do what is good. Let us live our lives in love for one another, bearing each other's burdens. Proclaim what is right, denounce what is evil. Hold those accountable that seek to divide the body and entice us to sin against our Lord. If we refuse to deny Him; if we remain faithful in Christ, then He proclaims us as those worthy of the calling. He will present us before the Father as those that fulfilled His good pleasure; and therefore fit to receive all that He promised those that love Him.